...comes in 148
Delicious
Flavors

Old Mr. Boston®

Deluxe Official Bartender's Guide

WARNER BOOKS

A Warner Communications Company

Mr. Boston Bartender's Guide

Warner Books Edition

1st printing January 1935. 2nd printing March 1935. 3rd printing October 1936. 4th printing (revised) September 1940. 5th printing October 1941. 6th printing November 1946. 7th printing December 1948. 8th printing September 1949. 9th printing February 1951. 10th printing April 1953. 11th printing December 1953. 12th printing (revised) July 1955. 13th printing September 1957. 14th printing May 1959. 15th printing December 1959. 16th printing (revised) August 1960. 17th printing January 1961. 18th printing June 1961. 19th printing September 1961. 20th printing October 1961. 21st printing December 1962. 22nd printing January 1963. 23rd printing August 1963. 24th printing October 1963. 25th printing November 1963. 26th printing December 1963. 27th printing May 1964. 28th printing November 1964. 29th printing January 1965. 30th printing April 1965. 31st printing May 1965. 32nd printing October 1965. 33rd printing November 1965. 34th printing January 1966. 35th printing February 1966. 36th printing August 1966. 37th printing January 1967. 38th printing February 1967. 39th printing May 1967. 40th printing September 1967. 41st printing January 1968. 42nd printing April 1968. 43rd printing May 1968. 44th printing November 1968. 45th printing January 1969. 46th printing February 1969. 47th printing November 1969. 48th printing December 1969. 49th printing April 1970. 50th printing February 1971. 51st printing October 1971. 52nd printing September 1972. 53rd printing (revised) June 1974. 54th printing August 1974. 55th printing April 1976. 56th printing January 1977. 57th printing January 1978. 58th printing September 1978. 59th printing January 1979. 60th printing September 1979. 61st printing November 1981. 62nd printing January 1982. 63rd printing November 1982. 64th printing December 1983.

This Warner Books Edition is published by arrangement with Glenmore Distilleries Company.

Warner Books, Inc., 666 Fifth Avenue, New York, N.Y. 10103

 A Warner Communications Company

Printed in the United States of America

Photography by Joyce Goldsmith, Warren Lynch, Photography, Inc., David Talbott, Norman Trigg and Mel Victor

Art Director William J. Cummings

Library of Congress Cataloging in Publication Data

Main entry under title:

Old Mr. Boston deluxe official bartender's guide.

   Reprint. Originally published: Boston: Mr. Boston Distiller Corp., 1979.
   1. Liquors. 2. Cocktails. 3. Alcoholic beverages.
I. Title: Deluxe official bartender's guide.
TX951.04 1981 641.8'74 81-2986
ISBN 0-446-37043-6 (U.S.A.) AACR2
ISBN 0-446-37153-X (Canada)

A New Dimension of Beverage Enjoyment

For both the amateur and professional mixologist, the Mr. Boston Bartender's Guide has, for many years, been recognized as the most complete and accurate reference for alcoholic beverage recipes. Since the first printing in 1935, over eight million copies have been distributed. It would be rare to find a bartender who did not have a Mr. Boston Bartender's Guide in his collection to assist him in fulfilling a request for an unusual cocktail or drink.

Mr. Boston, recognized for innovative achievements in the liquor industry, is proud of the status the Guide has achieved, but is not willing to rest on past laurels. Rather, the present Bar Guide represents the fruits of tremendous research in an effort to bring up to date this finest reference source available for bartending. The newly designed and revised hard-cover book now contains over 1000 recipes, including 400 new cocktail recipes, made easily accessible by fingertip indexing. A section has been set aside for a liquor dictionary with definitions of various alcoholic beverages in concise, understandable language. Bar hints are also offered, including descriptions of equipment, measurements, and other aids which contribute to the ultimate concoction of perfect drinks. In short, Mr. Boston has spared no expense in bringing you one of the finest and most authentic drink-recipe books ever published.

We at Mr. Boston, distributor of the largest line of fine liquors in the world, are delighted with the newest edition. We hope you have similar feelings.

Contents

A

ABBEY COCKTAIL
1½ oz. Old Mr. Boston Dry Gin
Juice ¼ Orange
1 dash Orange Bitters
Shake with ice and strain into cocktail glass. Add a maraschino cherry.

ABSINTHE COCKTAIL
1½ oz. Absinthe Substitute
2 tablespoons Water
1½ teaspoons Old Mr. Boston Anisette
1 dash Orange Bitters
Shake with ice and strain into cocktail glass.

ABSINTHE DRIP COCKTAIL
Pour 1½ oz. Absinthe Substitute into special drip glass or old-fashioned cocktail glass. Place cube of sugar over hole of drip spoon (or in silver tea strainer). Pack spoon or strainer with cracked ice, pour cold water to fill. When water has dripped through, drink is ready.

ABSINTHE SPECIAL COCKTAIL
1½ oz. Absinthe Substitute
1 oz. Water
¼ teaspoon Powdered Sugar
1 dash Orange Bitters
Shake with ice and strain into cocktail glass.

ACAPULCO
1½ oz. Old Mr. Boston Rum
1 tablespoon Lime Juice
1½ teaspoons Old Mr. Boston Triple Sec
1 teaspoon Sugar
1 teaspoon Egg White
Combine and shake all ingredients with ice and strain into old-fashioned glass over ice cubes. Add sprig of mint.

ADAM AND EVE
1 oz. Forbidden Fruit
1 oz. Old Mr. Boston Dry Gin
1 oz. Old Mr. Boston Five Star Brandy
1 dash Lemon Juice
Shake well with cracked ice and strain into cocktail glass.

ADONIS COCKTAIL
1 dash Orange Bitters
¾ oz. Sweet Vermouth
1½ oz. Dry Sherry
Stir with ice and strain into cocktail glass.

AFFINITY COCKTAIL
1 oz. Dry Vermouth
1 oz. Sweet Vermouth
1 oz. Desmond & Duff Scotch Whisky
3 dashes Orange Bitters
Stir with ice and strain into cocktail glass.

OLD Mr. BOSTON

AFTER DINNER COCKTAIL

1 oz. Old Mr. Boston Apricot
  Flavored Brandy
1 oz. Old Mr. Boston Triple
  Sec
Juice 1 Lime
*Shake with ice and strain into
cocktail glass. Leave lime in
glass.*

AFTER SUPPER COCKTAIL

1 oz. Old Mr. Boston Apricot Flavored Brandy
1 oz. Old Mr. Boston Triple
  Sec
½ teaspoon Lemon Juice
*Shake with ice and strain into
cocktail glass.*

A. J.

1½ oz. Applejack
1 oz. Grapefruit Juice
*Shake with ice and strain into
cocktail glass.*

ALABAMA FIZZ

Juice ½ Lemon
1 teaspoon Powdered Sugar
2 oz. Old Mr. Boston Dry Gin
*Shake well with cracked ice
and strain into highball glass
over two ice cubes. Fill with
carbonated water. Add two
sprigs of fresh mint.*

ALASKA COCKTAIL

2 dashes Orange Bitters
1½ oz. Old Mr. Boston Dry
  Gin
¾ oz. Chartreuse (Yellow)
*Stir with ice and strain into
cocktail glass.*

ALBEMARLE FIZZ

Juice ½ Lemon
1 teaspoon Powdered Sugar
2 oz. Old Mr. Boston Dry Gin
*Shake with ice and strain into
highball glass over two ice
cubes. Fill with carbonated
water. Add one teaspoon
raspberry syrup.*

ALEXANDER COCKTAIL No. 1

1 oz. Old Mr. Boston Dry Gin
1 oz. Old Mr. Boston Crème
  de Cacao (White)
1 oz. Sweet Cream
*Shake with ice and strain into
cocktail glass. Sprinkle nutmeg on top.*

ALEXANDER COCKTAIL No.2

1 oz. Old Mr. Boston Crème
  de Cacao (White)
1 oz. Old Mr. Boston Five
  Star Brandy
1 oz. Sweet Cream
*Shake with ice and strain into
cocktail glass. Sprinkle nutmeg on top.*

ALEXANDER'S SISTER COCKTAIL

1 oz. Old Mr. Boston Dry Gin
1 oz. Old Mr. Boston Crème
  de Menthe (Green)
1 oz. Sweet Cream
*Shake with ice and strain into
cocktail glass. Sprinkle nutmeg on top.*

ALFIE COCKTAIL
1½ oz. Old Mr. Boston
    Lemon Vodka
1 tablespoon Pineapple Juice
1 dash Mr. Boston Triple Sec
Shake with ice and strain into cocktail glass.

ALGONQUIN
1½ oz. Old Thompson
    Blended Whiskey
1 oz. Dry Vermouth
1 oz. Pineapple Juice
Shake with ice and strain into cocktail glass.

ALLEGHENY
1 oz. Kentucky Tavern Bourbon
1 oz. Dry Vermouth
1½ teaspoons Old Mr. Boston
    Blackberry Flavored
    Brandy
1½ teaspoons Lemon Juice
Shake with ice and strain into cocktail glass. Add a twist of lemon peel on top.

ALLEN COCKTAIL
1½ teaspoons Lemon Juice
¾ oz. Maraschino
1½ oz. Old Mr. Boston Dry
    Gin
Shake with ice and strain into cocktail glass.

ALLIES COCKTAIL
1 oz. Dry Vermouth
1 oz. Old Mr. Boston Dry Gin
½ teaspoon Kümmel
Stir with ice and strain into cocktail glass.

ALMERIA
1½ oz. Old Mr. Boston Rum
1 oz. Old Mr. Boston Coffee
    Flavored Brandy
1 Egg White
Shake all ingredients with cracked ice and strain into cocktail glass.

AMARETTO AND CREAM
1½ oz. Amaretto di Saronno
1½ oz. Sweet Cream
Shake well with cracked ice. Strain and serve in cocktail glass.

AMARETTO CAFÉ
Add 1 oz. Amaretto di Saronno to a cup of black coffee.

AMARETTO SOUR
1½ oz. Amaretto di Saronno
¾ oz. Lemon Juice
    (No Sugar)
Shake well with cracked ice and strain into sour glass. Garnish with slice of orange.

AMARETTO STINGER
1½ oz. Amaretto di Saronno
¾ oz. Mr. Boston Creme
    de Menthe (White)
Shake well with ice. Strain and serve in cocktail glass.

AMBROSIA
1 oz. Applejack
1 oz. Old Mr. Boston Five
    Star Brandy
1 dash Old Mr. Boston
    Triple Sec
Juice 1 Lemon
Champagne
Shake all ingredients except champagne. Pour contents into highball glass with cubed ice. Fill with champagne.

AMER PICON COCKTAIL

Juice 1 Lime
1 teaspoon Grenadine
1½ oz. Amer Picon
Shake with ice and strain into cocktail glass.

AMERICAN BEAUTY COCKTAIL

1 tablespoon Orange Juice
1 tablespoon Grenadine
½ oz. Dry Vermouth
½ oz. Old Mr. Boston
    Five Star Brandy
¼ teaspoon Old Mr. Boston
    Crème de Menthe (White)
Shake with ice and strain into cocktail glass and top with a little Port.

AMERICAN GROG

1 lump Sugar
Juice ¼ Lemon
1½ oz. Old Mr. Boston Rum
Pour ingredients into hot whiskey glass and fill with hot water. Stir.

AMERICANO

Pour 2 oz. Sweet Vermouth and 2 oz. Campari into highball glass over ice cubes. Fill with carbonated water and stir. Add twist of lemon peel.

ANDALUSIA

1½ oz. Dry Sherry
½ oz. Old Mr. Boston
    Five Star Brandy
½ oz. Old Mr. Boston Rum
Stir well with cracked ice and strain into cocktail glass.

ANGEL'S DELIGHT

1½ teaspoons Grenadine
1½ teaspoons Mr. Boston
    Triple Sec
1½ teaspoons Mr. Boston
    Sloe Gin
1½ teaspoons Sweet Cream
Pour carefully, in order given, into pousse-café glass so that each ingredient floats on preceding one without mixing.

ANGEL FACE

1 oz. Old Mr. Boston Dry Gin
½ oz. Old Mr. Boston
    Apricot Flavored Brandy
½ oz. Apple Brandy
Shake well with cracked ice and strain into cocktail glass.

ANGEL'S KISS

¼ oz. Mr. Boston Crème
    de Cacao (White)
¼ oz. Mr. Boston Sloe Gin
¼ oz. Mr. Boston Five
    Star Brandy
¼ oz. Sweet Cream
Pour ingredients carefully, in order given, so that they do not mix. Use pousse-café glass.

ANGEL'S TIP

¾ oz. Old Mr. Boston
    Crème de Cacao (White)
¼ oz. Sweet Cream
Float cream and insert toothpick in cherry and put on top. Use pousse-café glass.

OLD Mr. BOSTON

ANGEL'S WING
½ oz. Old Mr. Boston Crème de Cacao (White)
½ oz. Old Mr. Boston Five Star Brandy
1 tablespoon Sweet Cream
Pour ingredients carefully, in order given, so that they do not mix. Use pousse-café glass.

ANGLER'S COCKTAIL
2 dashes Angostura Bitters
3 dashes Orange bitters
1½ oz. Old Mr. Boston Dry Gin
1 dash Grenadine
Shake with cracked ice and pour into old-fashioned glass over ice cubes.

ANTE
1 oz. Apple Brandy
½ oz. Old Mr. Boston Triple Sec
1 oz. Dubonnet
Stir well with cracked ice and strain into cocktail glass.

ANTOINE SPECIAL
1½ oz. Dubonnet
1½ oz. Dry Vermouth
Float vermouth on top of chilled Dubonnet in a wine glass.

APPLE BLOW FIZZ
1 Egg White
Juice ½ Lemon
1 teaspoon Powdered Sugar
2 oz. Apple Brandy
Shake with ice and strain into highball glass with two ice cubes. Fill with carbonated water.

APPLE BRANDY COCKTAIL
1½ oz. Apple Brandy
1 teaspoon Grenadine
1 teaspoon Lemon Juice
Shake with ice and strain into cocktail glass.

APPLE BRANDY HIGHBALL
2 oz. Apple Brandy
Pour over ice cubes in a highball glass. Fill with ginger ale or carbonated water. Add twist of lemon peel, if desired, and stir.

APPLE BRANDY RICKEY
Juice ½ Lime
1½ oz. Apple Brandy
Fill highball glass with carbonated water and ice cubes. Leave lime in glass. Stir.

APPLE BRANDY SOUR
Juice ½ Lemon
½ teaspoon Powdered Sugar
2 oz. Apple Brandy
Shake with ice and strain into sour glass. Decorate with a half slice of lemon and a cherry.

APPLECAR

1 oz. Applejack
1 oz. Old Mr. Boston Triple Sec
1 oz. Lemon Juice
Shake with ice and strain into cocktail glass.

APPLEJACK PUNCH

2 qts. Applejack
4 oz. Grenadine
1 pint Orange Juice
Combine ingredients in punch bowl with large block of ice. Add 2 quarts ginger ale and slices of apple.

APPLE PIE COCKTAIL

¾ oz. Old Mr. Boston Rum
¾ oz. Sweet Vermouth
1 teaspoon Apple Flavored Brandy
½ teaspoon Grenadine
1 teaspoon Lemon Juice
Shake with ice and strain into cocktail glass.

APPLE RUM RICKEY

¾ oz. Applejack
¾ oz. Old Mr. Boston Rum
¼ Lime
Pour applejack and rum into highball glass over ice cubes. Fill with carbonated water. Squeeze lime and drop into glass. Stir.

APRICOT ANISE COLLINS

1½ oz. Old Mr. Boston Gin
½ oz. Old Mr. Boston Apricot Flavored Brandy
1½ teaspoons Old Mr. Boston Anisette
1 tablespoon Lemon Juice
Shake with ice and strain into collins glass over ice cubes. Fill with carbonated water and stir lightly. Garnish with slice of lemon.

APRICOT BRANDY RICKEY

Juice ½ Lime
2 oz. Old Mr. Boston Apricot Flavored Brandy
Pour into highball glass over ice cubes and fill with carbonated water. Drop rind of lime into glass. Stir.

APRICOT COCKTAIL

Juice ¼ Lemon
Juice ¼ Orange
1½ oz. Old Mr. Boston Apricot Flavored Brandy
1 teaspoon Old Mr. Boston Dry Gin
Shake with ice and strain into cocktail glass.

APRICOT COOLER

In a collins glass, dissolve ½ teaspoon powdered sugar and 2 oz. carbonated water. Stir and fill glass with cracked ice and add 2 oz. Old Mr. Boston Apricot Flavored Brandy. Fill with carbonated water or ginger ale and stir again. Insert spiral of orange or lemon peel (or both) and dangle end over rim of glass.

APRICOT FIZZ

Juice ½ Lemon
Juice ½ Lime
1 teaspoon Powdered Sugar
2 oz. Old Mr. Boston
    Apricot Flavored Brandy
Shake with cracked ice and strain into highball glass with two cubes ice. Fill with carbonated water.

APRICOT LADY

1¼ oz. Old Mr. Boston Rum
1 oz. Old Mr. Boston.
    Apricot Flavored Brandy
½ Teaspoon Old Mr. Boston
    Triple Sec
1 tablespoon Lime Juice
1 teaspoon Egg White
Shake all ingredients with ice and strain into old-fashioned glass over ice cubes. Add orange slice.

AQUARIUS

1½ oz. Old Thompson
    Blended Whiskey
½ oz. Old Mr. Boston Wild
    Cherry Flavored Brandy
1 oz. Cranberry Juice
Shake with ice and strain into old-fashioned glass on the rocks.

AQUEDUCT

1½ oz. Old Mr. Boston
    Vodka
1½ teaspoons Curaçao
1½ teaspoons Old Mr. Boston
    Apricot Flavored Brandy
1 tablespoon Lime Juice
Combine and shake all ingredients and strain into cocktail glass. Add a twist of orange peel.

ARISE MY LOVE

1 teaspoon Old Mr. Boston
    Crème de Menthe (Green)
Chilled Champagne
Put crème de menthe into champagne glass. Fill with champagne.

ARTILLERY

1½ oz. Old Mr. Boston Dry
    Gin
1½ teaspoons Sweet
    Vermouth
2 dashes Angostura Bitters
Stir with ice and strain into cocktail glass.

AUNT JEMIMA

½ oz. Old Mr. Boston
    Five Star Brandy
½ oz. Old Mr. Boston
    Crème de Cacao (White)
½ oz. Benedictine
Pour carefully in order given into a pousse-café glass so that ingredients do not mix.

B

B & B
½ oz. Benedictine
½ oz. Old Mr. Boston
  Five Star Brandy
*Use cordial glass and care-
fully float the brandy on top
of the Benedictine.*

BABBIE'S SPECIAL COCKTAIL
1 tablespoon Sweet Cream
1½ oz. Old Mr. Boston
  Apricot Flavored Brandy
¼ teaspoon Old Mr. Boston
  Dry Gin
*Shake with ice and strain into
cocktail glass.*

BACARDI COCKTAIL
1½ oz. Bacardi Rum
Juice ½ Lime
½ teaspoon Grenadine
*Shake with ice and strain into
cocktail glass.*

BACHELOR'S BAIT COCKTAIL
1½ oz. Old Mr. Boston Dry
  Gin
1 Egg White
1 dash Orange Bitters
½ teaspoon Grenadine
*Shake with ice and strain into
cocktail glass.*

BALTIMORE BRACER COCKTAIL
1 oz. Old Mr. Boston Anisette
1 oz. Old Mr. Boston Five
  Star Brandy
1 Egg White
*Shake with ice and strain into
cocktail glass.*

BALTIMORE EGGNOG
1 Whole Egg
1 teaspoon Powdered Sugar
1 oz. Old Mr. Boston Five
  Star Brandy
1 oz. Jamaica Rum
1 oz. Madeira
¾ cup Milk
*Shake well with ice and
strain into collins glass. Sprinkle nutmeg on top.*

BAMBOO COCKTAIL
1½ oz. Dry Sherry
¾ oz. Dry Vermouth
1 dash Orange Bitters
*Stir with ice and strain into
cocktail glass.*

BANANA DAIQUIRI
*Same as Frozen Daiquiri
Cocktail on page 59, but add
a sliced medium-size ripe banana.*

BANANA PUNCH

2 oz. Old Mr. Boston Vodka
1½ teaspoons Old Mr. Boston Apricot Flavored Brandy
Juice ½ Lime
Pour into collins glass filled with crushed ice. Add carbonated water and top with slices of banana and sprigs of mint.

BANSHEE

1 oz. Old Mr. Boston Crème de Banana
½ oz. Old Mr. Boston Crème de Cacao (White)
½ oz. Sweet Cream
Shake with cracked ice and strain into cocktail glass.

BARBARY COAST COCKTAIL

½ oz. Old Mr. Boston Dry Gin
½ oz. Old Mr. Boston Rum
½ oz. Old Mr. Boston Crème de Cacao
½ oz. Desmond & Duff Scotch Whisky
½ oz. Sweet Cream
Shake with ice and strain into cocktail glass.

BARNABY'S BUFFALO BLIZZARD*

1 oz. Mr. Boston Crème de Cacao (White)
¾ oz. Mr. Boston Vodka
1 oz. Galliano, vanilla ice cream
Dash Grenadine
Whipped cream
¾ cup milk
Shake or blend.

*Barnaby's Restaurant, Buffalo, N.Y.

BARON COCKTAIL

½ oz. Dry Vermouth
1½ oz. Old Mr. Boston Dry Gin
1½ teaspoons Old Mr. Boston Triple Sec
½ teaspoon Sweet Vermouth
Stir with ice and strain into cocktail glass. Add twist of lemon peel.

BARTON SPECIAL

½ oz. Applejack
¼ oz. Desmond & Duff Scotch Whisky
¼ oz. Old Mr. Boston Dry Gin
Shake with ice and strain into old-fashioned glass over ice cubes.

BEACHCOMBER

1½ oz. Old Mr. Boston Rum
½ oz. Lime Juice
½ oz. Old Mr. Boston Triple Sec
1 dash Maraschino
Shake with cracked ice and strain into cocktail glass, rimmed with lime juice and sugar.

BEADLESTONE COCKTAIL

1½ oz. Dry Vermouth
1½ oz. Desmond & Duff Scotch Whisky
Stir with ice and strain into cocktail glass.

BEALS COCKTAIL

1½ oz. Desmond & Duff Scotch Whisky
½ oz. Dry Vermouth
½ oz. Sweet Vermouth
Stir with ice and strain into cocktail glass.

BEAUTY SPOT COCKTAIL

1 teaspoon Orange Juice
½ oz. Sweet Vermouth
½ oz. Dry Vermouth
1 oz. Old Mr. Boston Dry
   Gin

Shake with ice and strain into cocktail glass, with a dash of Grenadine in bottom of glass.

BEER BUSTER

1½ oz. Old Mr. Boston 100
   proof Vodka
Ice-cold Beer
2 dashes Tabasco Sauce

Put Vodka in a highball glass and fill with beer or ale. Add Tabasco and stir lightly.

BELMONT COCKTAIL

2 oz. Old Mr. Boston Dry
   Gin
1 teaspoon Raspberry Syrup
¾ oz. Sweet Cream

Shake with ice and strain into cocktail glass.

BENNETT COCKTAIL

Juice ½ Lime
1½ oz. Old Mr. Boston Dry
   Gin
½ teaspoon Powdered Sugar
2 dashes Orange Bitters

Shake with ice and strain into cocktail glass.

BENTLEY

1½ oz. Apple Brandy
1 oz. Dubonnet

Stir with cracked ice and strain into cocktail glass. Add twist of lemon peel.

BERMUDA BOUQUET

Juice ¼ Orange
Juice ½ Lemon
1 teaspoon Powdered Sugar
1½ oz. Old Mr. Boston Dry
   Gin
1 oz. Old Mr. Boston Apricot
   Flavored Brandy
1 teaspoon Grenadine
½ teaspoon Old Mr. Boston
   Triple Sec

Shake with ice and strain into highball glass with ice cubes.

BERMUDA HIGHBALL

¾ oz. Old Mr. Boston Dry
   Gin
¾ oz. Old Mr. Boston Five
   Star Brandy
¾ oz. Dry Vermouth

Pour into highball glass over ice cubes. Fill with ginger ale or carbonated water. Add twist of lemon peel, if desired, and stir.

BERMUDA ROSE COCKTAIL

1¼ oz. Old Mr. Boston Dry
   Gin
1½ teaspoons Old Mr. Boston
   Apricot Flavored Brandy
1½ teaspoons Grenadine

Shake with ice and strain into cocktail glass.

BETSY ROSS COCKTAIL

1½ oz. Old Mr. Boston Five
   Star Brandy
1½ oz. Port
1 dash Old Mr. Boston
   Triple Sec

Stir with cracked ice and strain into cocktail glass.

◄ *Mr. Boston Flavored Brandies: 70 Proof—Coffee, Blackberry, Ginger, Peach, Wild Cherry and Apricot.*

BETWEEN-THE-SHEETS COCKTAIL

Juice ¼ Lemon
½ oz. Old Mr. Boston Five Star Brandy
½ oz. Old Mr. Boston Triple Sec
½ oz. Old Mr. Boston Rum
Shake with ice and strain into cocktail glass.

BIFFY COCKTAIL

Juice ½ Lemon
1 tablespoon Swedish Punch
1½ oz. Old Mr. Boston Dry Gin
Shake with ice and strain into cocktail glass.

BIJOU COCKTAIL

¾ oz. Old Mr. Boston Dry Gin
¾ oz. Chartreuse (Green)
¾ oz. Sweet Vermouth
1 dash Orange Bitters
Stir with ice and strain into cocktail glass. Add cherry on top.

BILLY TAYLOR

Juice ½ Lime
2 oz. Old Mr. Boston Dry Gin
Fill collins glass with carbonated water and ice cubes. Stir.

BIRD-OF-PARADISE FIZZ

Juice ½ Lemon
1 teaspoon Powdered Sugar
1 Egg White
1 teaspoon Grenadine
2 oz. Old Mr. Boston Dry Gin
Shake with ice and strain into highball glass over two ice cubes. Fill with carbonated water.

BISHOP

Juice ¼ Lemon
Juice ¼ Orange
1 teaspoon Powdered Sugar
Shake with ice and strain into highball glass. Add two ice cubes, fill with burgundy and stir well. Decorate with fruits.

BITTERS HIGHBALL

Fill highball glass with ¾ oz. Bitters, ice cubes, and ginger ale or carbonated water. Add twist of lemon peel, if desired, and stir.

BITTERSWEET

1½ oz. Sweet Vermouth
1½ oz. Dry Vermouth
1 dash Angostura Bitters
1 dash Orange Bitters
Stir with cracked ice and strain into cocktail glass. Add twist of orange peel.

BLACK DEVIL

2 oz. Old Mr. Boston Rum
½ oz. Dry Vermouth
Stir with cracked ice and strain into cocktail glass. Add black olive.

BLACK HAWK COCKTAIL

1¼ oz. Old Thompson
    Blended Whiskey
1¼ Old Mr. Boston
    Sole Gin
Stir with ice and strain into cocktail glass. Serve with a cherry.

BLACKJACK

1 oz. Kirschwasser
½ oz. Old Mr. Boston
    Five Star Brandy
1 oz. Coffee
Shake with cracked ice and strain into old-fashioned glass over ice cubes.

BLACK MAGIC

1½ oz. Old Mr. Boston
    Vodka
¾ oz. Expresso Coffee
    Liqueur
1 dash Lemon Juice
Stir and serve in old-fashioned glass over ice cubes and add a twist of lemon peel.

BLACK MARIA

2 oz. Old Mr. Boston
    Coffee Flavored Brandy
2 oz. Old Mr. Boston Rum
4 oz. Strong Black Coffee
2 Teaspoons Powdered Sugar
Stir in brandy snifter and add cracked ice.

BLACK RUSSIAN

1½ oz. Old Mr. Boston
    Vodka
¾ oz. Old Mr. Boston Coffee
    Flavored Brandy
Pour over ice cubes in old-fashioned cocktail glass.

BLACK SOMBRERO

See Sombrero recipe on page 138.

BLACKTHORN

1½ oz. Old Mr. Boston Sloe
    Gin
1 oz. Sweet Vermouth
Stir with ice and strain into cocktail glass. Add twist of lemon peel.

BLACK VELVET

5 oz. Chilled Stout
5 oz. Chilled Champagne
Pour very carefully, in order given, into champagne glass so that the stout and champagne don't mix.

BLANCHE

1 oz. Old Mr. Boston
    Anisette
1 oz. Old Mr. Boston
    Triple Sec
½ oz. Curaçao (White)
Shake with cracked ice and strain into cocktail glass.

BLARNEY STONE COCKTAIL
2 oz. Irish Whisky
½ teaspoon Absinthe Substitute
½ teaspoon Old Mr. Boston Triple Sec
¼ teaspoon Maraschino
1 dash Bitters
Shake with ice and strain into cocktail glass. Add twist of orange peel and an olive.

BLOOD-AND-SAND COCKTAIL
1 tablespoon Orange Juice
½ oz. Desmond & Duff Scotch Whisky
½ oz. Old Mr. Boston Wild Cherry Flavored Brandy
½ oz. Sweet Vermouth
Shake with ice and strain into cocktail glass.

BLOOD BRONX COCKTAIL
1½ oz. Old Mr. Boston Dry Gin
1½ teaspoons Dry Vermouth
Juice ¼ Blood Orange
Shake with ice and strain into cocktail glass.

BLOODHOUND COCKTAIL
½ oz. Dry Vermouth
½ oz. Sweet Vermouth
1 oz. Old Mr. Boston Dry Gin
Shake with ice and strain into cocktail glass. Decorate with two or three crushed strawberries.

BLOODY MARIA
1 oz. Gavilan Tequila
2 oz. Tomato Juice
1 dash Lemon Juice
1 dash Tabasco Sauce
1 dash Celery Salt
Shake all ingredients with cracked ice. Strain into old-fashioned glass over ice cubes. Add slice of lemon.

BLOODY MARY
1½ oz. Old Mr. Boston Vodka
3 oz. Tomato Juice
1 dash Lemon Juice
½ teaspoon Worcestershire Sauce
2 or 3 drops Tabasco Sauce
Pepper and Salt
Shake with ice and strain into old-fashioned glass over ice cubes. A wedge of lime may be added.

BLUE BIRD
1½ oz. Old Mr. Boston Dry Gin
½ oz. Old Mr. Boston Triple Sec
1 dash Bitters
Stir with ice cubes and strain into cocktail glass. Add twist of lemon peel and a cherry.

BLUE BLAZER

Use two large silver-plated mugs, with handles.
2½ oz. Old Thompson
    Blended Whiskey
2½ oz. Boiling Water
Put the whiskey into one mug, and the boiling water into the other. Ignite the whiskey and, while blazing, mix both ingredients by pouring them four or five times from one mug to the other. If well done, this will have the appearance of a continuous stream of liquid fire. Sweeten with 1 teaspoon of powdered sugar and serve with a twist of lemon peel. Serve in a 4-oz. hot whiskey glass.

BLUE DEVIL COCKTAIL

1 oz. Old Mr. Boston Dry Gin
Juice ½ Lemon or 1 Lime
1 tablespoon Maraschino
½ teaspoon Blue Curacao
Shake with ice and strain into cocktail glass.

BLUE MONDAY COCKTAIL

1½ oz. Old Mr. Boston
    Vodka
¾ oz. Old Mr. Boston Triple
    Sec
1 dash Blue Vegetable
    Coloring
Stir with ice and strain into cocktail glass.

BLUE MOON COCKTAIL

1½ oz. Old Mr. Boston
    Dry Gin
¾ oz. Blue Curacao
Stir with ice and strain into cocktail glass. Add twist of lemon peel.

BOBBY BURNS COCKTAIL

1½ oz. Sweet Vermouth
1½ oz. Desmond & Duff
    Scotch Whisky
1¼ teaspoons Benedictine
Stir with ice and strain into cocktail glass. Add twist of lemon peel.

BOCCIE BALL

1½ oz. Amaretto di Saronno
1½ oz. Orange Juice
2 oz. Club Soda
Serve in a highball glass with ice.

BOLERO COCKTAIL

1½ oz. Old Mr. Boston Rum
¾ oz. Apple Brandy
¼ teaspoon Sweet Vermouth
Stir well with cracked ice and strain into cocktail glass.

BOMBAY COCKTAIL

½ oz. Dry Vermouth
½ oz. Sweet Vermouth
1 oz. Old Mr. Boston
    Five Star Brandy
¼ teaspoon Absinthe
    Substitute
½ teaspoon Old Mr. Boston
    Triple Sec
Stir with ice and strain into cocktail glass.

OLD Mr. BOSTON

BOMBAY PUNCH

Juice 12 Lemons
*Add enough powdered sugar
to sweeten the lemon juice.
Pour over a large block of
ice in punch bowl and stir.
Then add:*
1 qt. Old Mr. Boston
    Five Star Brandy
1 qt. Dry Sherry
½ cup Maraschino
½ cup Old Mr. Boston
    Triple Sec
4 bottles Chilled Champagne
2 qts. Chilled Carbonated
    Water
*Stir well and decorate with
fruits in season. Serve in
punch glasses.*

BOOMERANG

1 oz. Dry Vermouth
1½ oz. Old Mr. Boston Dry
    Gin
1 dash Bitters
1 dash Maraschino
*Stir with ice cubes and strain
into cocktail glass. Add twist
of lemon peel.*

BORINQUEN

1½ oz. Old Mr. Boston Rum
1 tablespoon Passion Fruit
    Syrup
1 oz. Lime Juice
1 oz. Orange Juice
1 teaspoon 151 Proof Rum
*Put half a cup of crushed ice
into blender. Add all ingredients and blend at low speed.
Pour into old-fashioned glass.*

BOSOM CARESSER

1 oz. Old Mr. Boston
    Five Star Brandy
1 oz. Madeira
½ oz. Old Mr. Boston
    Triple Sec

BOOM BOOM PUNCH

2 qts. Old Mr. Boston Rum
1 qt. Orange Juice
1 fifth Sweet Vermouth
1 bottle Chilled Champagne
*Pour into punch bowl over
large block of ice all ingredients except champagne.
Stir. Add champagne on top.
Decorate with sliced bananas.*

*Stir with cracked ice and
strain into cocktail glass.*

BOSTON BULLET

*See Special Martini Section
on pages 173 and 174.*

BOSTON COCKTAIL

¾ oz. Old Mr. Boston Dry Gin
¾ oz. Old Mr. Boston Apricot Flavored Brandy
Juice ¼ Lemon
1½ teaspoons Grenadine
Shake with ice and strain into cocktail glass.

BOSTON COOLER

Into collins glass, put the juice of ½ lemon, 1 teaspoon powdered sugar, and 2 oz. carbonated water. Stir. Then fill glass with cracked ice and add
2 oz. Old Mr. Boston Rum
Fill with carbonated water or ginger ale and stir again. Add spiral of orange or lemon peel (or both) and dangle end over rim of glass.

BOSTON GOLD

1 oz. Old Mr. Boston Vodka
½ oz. Old Mr. Boston Crème de Banana
Orange Juice
Pour vodka and banana liqueur over ice cubes in highball glass. Fill with orange juice and stir.

BOSTON SIDECAR COCKTAIL

¾ oz. Old Mr. Boston Five Star Brandy
¾ oz. Old Mr. Boston Rum
¾ oz. Old Mr. Boston Triple Sec
Juice ½ Lime
Shake with ice and strain into cocktail glass.

BOSTON SOUR

Juice ½ Lemon
1 teaspoon Powdered Sugar
2 oz. Old Thompson Blended Whiskey
1 Egg White
Shake with cracked ice and strain into sour glass. Add slice of lemon and a cherry.

BOURBON HIGHBALL

Fill highball glass with 2 oz. Old Kentucky Tavern Bourbon Whiskey, ginger ale or carbonated water, and ice cubes. Add twist of lemon peel, if desired, and stir.

BRANDIED MADEIRA

1 oz. Old Mr. Boston Five Star Brandy
1 oz. Madeira
½ oz. Dry Vermouth
Stir with cracked ice and strain into old-fashioned glass over ice cubes. Add a twist of lemon peel.

BRANDIED PORT

1 oz. Old Mr. Boston Five Star Brandy
1 oz. Tawny Port
1 tablespoon Lemon Juice
1 teaspoon Maraschino
Shake all ingredients and strain into old-fashioned glass with ice cubes. Add slice of orange.

BRANDY AND SODA

Pour 2 oz. Old Mr. Boston Five Star Brandy into collins glass with ice cubes. Add carbonated water.

OLD Mr. BOSTON

BRANTINI

1½ oz. Old Mr. Boston
    Five Star Brandy
1 oz. Old Mr. Boston Dry Gin
1 dash Dry Vermouth
Stir with cracked ice and strain into old-fashioned glass with cubed ice. Add a twist of lemon peel.

BRANDY BLAZER

1 lump Sugar
1 piece Orange Peel
1 piece Lemon Peel
2 oz. Old Mr. Boston
    Five Star Brandy
Combine ingredients in old-fashioned cocktail glass. Light the liquid with match, stir with long spoon for a few seconds, and strain into hot whiskey glass.

BRANDY COBBLER

Dissolve one teaspoon powdered sugar in 2 oz. carbonated water. Fill 10 oz. goblet with shaved ice.
Add 2 oz. Old Mr. Boston
    Five Star Brandy
Stir well and decorate with fruits in season. Serve with straws.

BRANDY COCKTAIL

2 oz. Old Mr. Boston
    Five Star Brandy
¼ teaspoon Sugar Syrup
2 dashes Bitters
Stir with ice and strain into cocktail glass. Add a twist of lemon peel.

BRANDY COLLINS

Juice ½ Lemon
1 teaspoon Powdered Sugar
2 oz. Old Mr. Boston
    Five Star Brandy
Shake with cracked ice and strain into collins glass. Add cubes of ice, fill with carbonated water, and stir. Decorate with slice of orange or lemon and a cherry. Serve with straws.

BRANDY CASSIS

1½ oz. Old Mr. Boston
    Five Star Brandy
1 oz. Lemon Juice
1 dash Mr. Boston
    Crème de Cassis
Shake with cracked ice and strain into cocktail glass. Add twist of lemon peel.

OLD Mr. BOSTON

BRANDY CRUSTA COCKTAIL

Moisten the edge of a cocktail glass with lemon and dip into sugar. Cut the rind of half a lemon in a spiral and place in glass.

1 teaspoon Maraschino
1 dash Bitters
1 teaspoon Lemon Juice
½ oz. Old Mr. Boston
    Triple Sec
2 oz. Old Mr. Boston
    Five Star Brandy

Stir above ingredients with ice and strain into sugar-rimmed glass. Add slice of orange.

BRANDY DAISY

Juice ½ Lemon
½ teaspoon Powdered Sugar
1 teaspoon Raspberry Syrup
    or Grenadine
2 oz. Old Mr. Boston
    Five Star Brandy

Shake with ice and strain into stein or 8 oz. metal cup. Add cubes of ice and decorate with fruit.

BRANDY EGGNOG

1 Whole Egg
1 teaspoon Powdered Sugar
2 oz. Old Mr. Boston
    Five Star Brandy

Shake with ice and strain into collins glass. Fill glass with milk. Sprinkle nutmeg on top.

BRANDY FIX

Mix juice of half a lemon, 1 teaspoon powdered sugar, and 1 teaspoon water in a highball glass. Stir. Then fill glass with shaved ice and

2½ oz. Old Mr. Boston
    Five Star Brandy.

Stir, add slice of lemon. Serve with straws.

BRANDY FIZZ

Juice ½ Lemon
1 teaspoon Powdered Sugar
2 oz. Old Mr. Boston
    Five Star Brandy

Shake with cracked ice and strain into highball glass over two ice cubes. Fill with carbonated water.

BRANDY FLIP

1 Whole Egg
1 teaspoon Powdered Sugar
1½ oz. Old Mr. Boston
    Five Star Brandy
2 teaspoons Sweet Cream
    (if desired)
Shake with ice and strain into flip glass. Sprinkle a little nutmeg on top.

BRANDY GUMP COCKTAIL

1½ oz. Old Mr. Boston
    Five Star Brandy
Juice ½ Lemon
½ teaspoon Grenadine
Shake with ice and strain into cocktail glass.

BRANDY HIGHBALL

In a highball glass pour 2 oz. Old Mr. Boston Five Star Brandy, over ice cubes and fill with ginger ale or carbonated water. Add twist of lemon peel, if desired, and stir gently.

BRANDY JULEP

Into collins glass put 1 teaspoon powdered sugar, five or six leaves of fresh mint, and 2½ oz. Old Mr. Boston Five Star Brandy.
Then fill glass with finely shaved ice, and stir until mint rises to top, being careful not to bruise the leaves. (Do not hold glass with hand while stirring.) Decorate with slice of pineapple, orange, or lemon and a cherry. Serve with straws.

BRANDY MILK PUNCH

1 teaspoon Powdered Sugar
2 oz. Old Mr. Boston
    Five Star Brandy
1 cup Milk
Shake with ice, strain into collins glass, and sprinkle nutmeg on top.

BRANDY PUNCH

Juice 1 dozen Lemons
Juice 4 Oranges
Add enough sugar to sweeten and mix with:
1 cup Grenadine
1 qt. Carbonated Water
Pour over large block of ice in punch bowl and stir well. Then add:
1 cup Old Mr. Boston
    Triple Sec
2 qts. Old Mr. Boston
    Five Star Brandy
2 cups Tea (optional)
Stir well and decorate with fruits in season. Serve in punch glasses.

BRANDY SANGAREE

Dissolve ½ teaspoon powdered sugar in 1 teaspoon of water, and add
2 oz. Old Mr. Boston
    Five Star Brandy.
Pour into highball glass over ice cubes. Fill with carbonated water. Stir. Float a tablespoon of Port on top and sprinkle lightly with nutmeg.

BRANDY SLING

Dissolve 1 teaspoon powdered sugar in teaspoon of water and juice ½ Lemon. Add
2 oz. Old Mr. Boston
    Five Star Brandy.
Serve in old-fashioned cocktail glass with cubed ice and twist of lemon peel.

BRANDY SMASH

Muddle 1 lump sugar with 1 oz. carbonated water and 4 sprigs of fresh mint. Add
2 oz. Old Mr. Boston
    Five Star Brandy.
Add cubes of ice. Stir and decorate with a slice of orange and a cherry. Add a twist of lemon peel on top. Use old-fashioned cocktail glass.

BRANDY SOUR

Juice ½ Lemon
½ teaspoon Powdered Sugar
2 oz. Old Mr. Boston
    Five Star Brandy
Shake with ice and strain into sour glass. Decorate with a half slice of lemon and a cherry.

BRANDY SQUIRT

1½ oz. Old Mr. Boston
    Five Star Brandy
1 tablespoon Powdered Sugar
1 teaspoon Raspberry Syrup
    or Grenadine
Shake with ice and strain into highball glass and fill with carbonated water. Decorate with stick of pineapple and strawberries.

BRANDY SWIZZLE

Made same as Gin Swizzle (see page 64), using
2 oz. Old Mr. Boston
    Five Star Brandy

BRANDY TODDY

In an old-fashioned glass dissolve:
½ teaspoon Powdered Sugar
1 teaspoon Water
Add:
2 oz. Old Mr. Boston
    Five Star Brandy
1 Ice Cube
Stir and add a twist of lemon peel on top.

OLD Mr. BOSTON

BRANDY TODDY (HOT)

Put lump of sugar into hot whiskey glass and fill two-thirds with boiling water. Add 2 oz. Old Mr. Boston Five Star Brandy.
Stir and decorate with slice of lemon. Sprinkle nutmeg on top.

BRANDY VERMOUTH COCKTAIL

½ oz. Sweet Vermouth
2 oz. Old Mr. Boston Five Star Brandy
1 dash Bitters
Stir with ice and strain into cocktail glass.

BRAZIL COCKTAIL

1½ oz. Dry Vermouth
1½ oz. Dry Sherry
1 dash Bitters
¼ teaspoon Absinthe Substitute
Stir with ice and strain into cocktail glass.

BREAKFAST EGGNOG

1 Whole Egg
½ oz. Old Mr. Boston Triple Sec
2 oz. Old Mr. Boston Apricot Flavored Brandy
6 oz. Milk
Shake well with cracked ice and strain into collins glass. Sprinkle nutmeg on top.

BRIGHTON PUNCH

¾ oz. Old Kentucky Tavern Bourbon Whiskey
¾ oz. Old Mr. Boston Five Star Brandy
¾ oz. Benedictine
Juice ½ Orange
Juice ½ Lemon
Shake with ice and pour into collins glass nearly filled with shaved ice. Then fill with car-bonated water and stir gently. Decorate with orange and lemon slices and serve with straw.

BROKEN SPUR COCKTAIL

¾ oz Sweet Vermouth
1½ oz. Port
¼ teaspoon Old Mr. Boston Triple Sec
Stir with ice and strain into cockail glass.

BRONX COCKTAIL

1 oz. Old Mr. Boston Dry Gin
½ oz. Dry Vermouth
½ oz. Sweet Vermouth
Juice ¼ Orange
Shake with ice and strain into cocktail glass. Serve with slice of orange.

BRONX COCKTAIL (DRY)

1 oz. Old Mr. Boston Dry Gin
1 oz. Dry Vermouth
Juice ¼ Orange
Shake with ice and strain into cocktail glass. Serve with slice of orange.

BRONX GOLDEN COCKTAIL

Same as Bronx Cocktail with the addition of one egg yolk. Use flip glass.

BRONX SILVER COCKTAIL
Juice ½ Orange
1 Egg White
½ oz. Dry Vermouth
1 oz. Old Mr. Boston Dry Gin
Shake with ice and strain into flip glass.

BRONX TERRACE COCKTAIL
1½ oz. Old Mr. Boston
    Dry Gin
1½ oz. Dry Vermouth
Juice ½ Lime
Shake with ice and strain into cocktail glass. Add a cherry.

BROWN COCKTAIL
¾ oz. Old Mr. Boston
    Dry Gin
¾ oz. Old Mr. Boston Rum
¾ oz. Dry Vermouth
Stir with ice and strain into cocktail glass.

BUCK JONES
1½ oz. Old Mr. Boston Rum
1 oz. Sweet Sherry
Juice ½ Lime
Pour ingredients into highball glass over ice cubes and stir. Fill with ginger ale.

BUCKS FIZZ
Pour 2 oz. orange juice in a collins glass over two cubes of ice, fill with champagne, and stir very gently.

BULLDOG COCKTAIL
1½ oz. Old Mr. Boston Wild
    Cherry Flavored Brandy
¾ oz. Old Mr. Boston
    Dry Gin
Juice ½ Lime
Shake with ice and strain into cocktail glass.

BULLDOG HIGHBALL
Juice ½ Orange
2 oz. Old Mr. Boston Dry Gin
Pour into highball glass over ice cubes and fill with ginger ale. Stir.

BULL SHOT
1½ oz. Old Mr. Boston
    Vodka
3 oz. Chilled Beef Bouillon
1 dash Worcestershire Sauce
1 dash Salt and Pepper
Shake with cracked ice and strain into old-fashioned glass.

BULL'S EYE
1 oz. Old Mr. Boston
    Five Star Brandy
2 oz. Hard Cider
Pour into highball glass over ice cubes and fill with ginger ale. Stir.

27

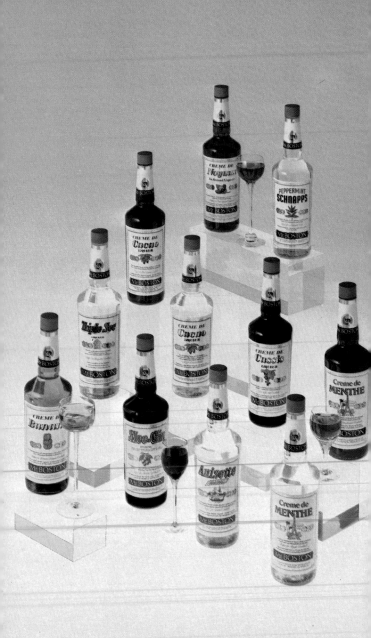

BULL'S MILK

1 teaspoon Powdered Sugar
1 oz. Old Mr. Boston Rum
1½ oz. Old Mr. Boston
Five Star Brandy
1 cup Milk
Shake with ice and strain into collins glass. Sprinkle nutmeg and pinch of cinnamon on top.

BURGUNDY BISHOP

Juice ¼ Lemon
1 teaspoon Powdered Sugar
1 oz. Old Mr. Boston Rum
Shake with ice and strain into highball glass over ice cubes. Fill with burgundy wine and stir. Decorate with fruits.

BUSHRANGER

1½ oz. Old Mr. Boston Rum
1 oz. Dubonnet
1 dash Bitters
Stir with cracked ice and strain into cocktail glass.

BUTTON HOOK COCKTAIL

½ oz. Old Mr. Boston
Crème de Menthe (White)
½ oz. Old Mr. Boston
Apricot Flavored Brandy
½ oz. Absinthe Substitute
½ oz. Old Mr. Boston
Five Star Brandy
Shake with ice and strain into cocktail glass.

Mr. Boston Cordials: Anisette, Creme de Banana, Creme de Cacao White & Brown, Creme de Menthe White & Green, Creme de Noyaux, Peppermint Schnapps, Triple Sec, 54 Proof, Creme de Cassis, 35 Proof and Sloe Gin, 60 Proof

29

CABARET COCKTAIL

1½ oz. Old Mr. Boston
    Dry Gin
2 dashes Bitters
½ teaspoon Dry Vermouth
¼ teaspoon Benedictine
Stir with ice and strain into cocktail glass. Serve with a cherry.

CABLEGRAM HIGHBALL

Juice ½ Lemon
1 teaspoon Powdered Sugar
2 oz. Old Thompson
    Blended Whiskey
Stir with ice cubes in highball glass and fill with ginger ale.

CADIZ

¾ oz. Dry Sherry
¾ oz. Old Mr. Boston Blackberry Flavored Brandy
½ oz. Old Mr. Boston
    Triple Sec
1 tablespoon Sweet Cream
Shake with ice and strain into old-fashioned glass over ice cubes.

CAFÉ DE PARIS COCKTAIL

1 Egg White
1 teaspoon Absinthe
    Substitute
1 teaspoon Sweet Cream
1½ oz. Old Mr. Boston
    Dry Gin
Shake with ice and strain into cocktail glass.

CAFÉ ROYALE

Put cube of sugar, well soaked with Old Mr. Boston Five Star Brandy, *in teaspoon and hold so that it will rest on top of one cup of hot black coffee and ignite. Hold until flame burns out. Drop contents in coffee.*

CALEDONIA

1 oz. Old Mr. Boston
    Crème de Cacao
1 oz. Old Mr. Boston
    Five Star Brandy
1 oz. Milk
1 Egg Yolk
Shake well with ice and strain into old-fashioned glass over ice cubes. Sprinkle cinnamon on top.

CALIFORNIA LEMONADE
Juice 1 Lemon
Juice 1 Lime
1 tablespoon Powdered Sugar
2 oz. Old Thompson
    Blended Whiskey
¼ teaspoon Grenadine
Shake with ice and strain into collins glass over shaved ice. Fill with carbonated water and decorate with slices of orange and lemon, and a cherry. Serve with straws.

CALM VOYAGE
½ oz. Strega
½ oz. Old Mr. Boston Rum
1 tablespoon Passion Fruit
    Syrup
2 teaspoons Lemon Juice
½ Egg White
Put all ingredients in blender with half a cup of crushed ice. Blend at low speed and pour into champagne glass.

CAMERON'S KICK COCKTAIL
¾ oz. Desmond & Duff
    Scotch Whisky
¾ oz. Irish Whisky
Juice ¼ Lemon
2 dashes Orange Bitters
Shake with ice and strain into cocktail glass.

CANADIAN CHERRY
1½ oz. Old Mr. Boston Five
    Star Canadian Whisky
½ oz. Old Mr. Boston Wild
    Cherry Flavored Brandy
1½ teaspoons Lemon Juice
1½ teaspoons Orange Juice
Shake all ingredients and strain into old-fashioned glass over ice cubes. Moisten glass rim with cherry brandy.

CANADIAN COCKTAIL
1½ oz. Old Mr. Boston Five
    Star Canadian Whisky
1 dash Angostura Bitters
1½ teaspoons Old Mr.
    Boston Triple Sec
1 teaspoon Powdered Sugar
Shake with ice and strain into cocktail glass.

CANADIAN PINEAPPLE
1½ oz. Old Mr. Boston Five
    Star Canadian Whisky
1 teaspoon Pineapple Juice
1 tablespoon Lemon Juice
½ teaspoon Maraschino
Shake with ice and strain into old-fashioned glass over ice cubes. Add stick of pineapple.

CANADO SALUDO
1½ oz. Old Mr. Boston Rum
1 oz. Orange Juice
1 oz. Pineapple Juice
5 dashes Lemon Juice
5 dashes Grenadine
5 dashes Angostura Bitters
Serve in a 6-oz. glass with pineapple slices, orange slice, and a cherry over ice cubes.

OLD Mr. BOSTON

CANAL STREET DAISY

Juice ¼ Lemon
Juice ¼ Orange
1 oz. Old Thompson
    Blended Whiskey
Pour all ingredients into a collins glass over ice cubes. Add carbonated water and orange slice.

CAPE CODDER

1½ oz. Old Mr. Boston Vodka
  or Old Mr. Boston Rum
3 oz. Cranberry Juice
Juice ½ Lime (if desired)
May be served on the rocks in old-fashioned glass or high-ball glass with cubes of ice and carbonated water. Stir.

CAPPUCINO COCKTAIL

¾ oz. Old Mr. Boston
    Coffee Flavored Brandy
¾ oz. Old Mr. Boston Vodka
¾ oz. Sweet Cream
*Shake well with ice. **Strain** into cocktail glass.*

CAPRI

¾ oz. Old Mr. Boston
    Crème de Cacao (White)
¾ oz. Old Mr. Boston
    Crème de Banana
¾ oz. Sweet Cream
Shake with ice and strain into old-fashioned glass over ice cubes.

CARA SPOSA

1 oz. Old Mr. Boston Coffee
    Flavored Brandy
1 oz. Old Mr. Boston
    Triple Sec
½ oz. Sweet Cream
Shake with ice and strain into cocktail glass.

CARDINAL PUNCH

Juice 1 dozen Lemons
Add enough powdered sugar to sweeten. Pour over large block of ice in punch bowl and stir well. Then add:
1 pt. Old Mr. Boston
    Five Star Brandy
1 pt. Old Mr. Boston Rum
1 split Champagne
2 qts. Claret
1 qt. Carbonated Water
½ pt. Sweet Vermouth
1 pt. Strong Tea (optional)
Stir well and decorate with fruits in season. Serve in punch glasses.

OLD Mr. BOSTON

CARIBBEAN CHAMPAGNE

½ teaspoon Old Mr. Boston Rum
½ teaspoon Old Mr. Boston Crème de Banana
Chilled Champagne
Pour rum and banana liqueur into champagne glass. Fill with champagne and stir lightly. Add slice of banana.

CARROL COCKTAIL

1½ oz. Old Mr. Boston Five Star Brandy
¾ oz. Sweet Vermouth
Stir with ice and strain into cocktail glass. Serve with a cherry.

CARUSO

1½ oz. Old Mr. Boston Dry Gin
1 oz. Dry Vermouth
½ oz. Old Mr. Boston Crème de Menthe (Green)
Stir with ice and strain into cocktail glass.

CASA BLANCA

2 oz. Old Mr. Boston Rum
1½ teaspoons Lime Juice
1½ teaspoons Old Mr. Boston Triple Sec
1½ teaspoons Maraschino
Shake with ice and strain into cocktail glass.

CASINO COCKTAIL

2 dashes Orange Bitters
¼ teaspoon Maraschino
¼ teaspoon Lemon Juice
2 oz. Old Mr. Boston Dry Gin
Shake with ice and strain into cocktail glass. Serve with a cherry.

CHAMPAGNE COCKTAIL

1 lump Sugar
2 dashes Bitters
Place in champagne glass and fill with chilled champagne. Add a twist of lemon peel.

CHAMPAGNE CUP

4 teaspoons Powdered Sugar
6 oz. Carbonated Water
1 oz. Old Mr. Boston Triple Sec
2 oz. Old Mr. Boston Five Star Brandy
Fill large glass pitcher with cubes of ice and the above ingredients. Add 1 pt. chilled champagne. Stir well and decorate with as many fruits as available and also rind of cucumber inserted on each side of pitcher. Top with small bunch of mint sprigs. Serve in claret glasses.

CHAMPAGNE PUNCH

Juice 1 dozen Lemons
Add enough powdered sugar to sweeten. Pour over large block of ice in punch bowl and stir well. Then add:
1 cup Maraschino
1 cup Old Mr. Boston
    Triple Sec
1 pt. Old Mr. Boston
    Five Star Brandy
2 bottles Champagne
1 pt. Carbonated Water
1 pt. Strong Tea (optional)
Stir well and decorate with fruits in season. Serve in punch glasses.

CHAMPAGNE SHERBET PUNCH

2 bottles Champagne
1 bottle Sauterne
1 qt. Lemon or Pineapple
    Sherbet
Put sherbet in punch bowl. Add sauterne and champagne. Decorate with lemon slices or pineapple chunks.

CHAMPAGNE VELVET

See Black Velvet recipe on page 15.

CHAMPS ELYSÉES COCKTAIL

1 oz. Old Mr. Boston
    Five Star Brandy
½ oz. Chartreuse (Yellow)
Juice ¼ Lemon
½ teaspoon Powdered Sugar
1 dash Bitters
Shake with ice and strain into cocktail glass.

CHAPALA

1½ oz. Gavilan Tequila
1 tablespoon Orange Juice
1 tablespoon Lemon Juice
1 dash Orange Flower Water
2 teaspoons Grenadine
Shake with ice and strain into old-fashioned glass over ice cubes. Add slice of orange.

CHAPEL HILL

1½ oz. Old Kentucky Tavern
    Bourbon Whiskey
½ oz. Old Mr. Boston Triple
    Sec
1 tablespoon Lemon Juice
Shake with ice and strain into cocktail glass. Add twist of orange peel.

35

OLD Mr. BOSTON

CHARLES COCKTAIL
1½ oz. Sweet Vermouth
1½ oz. Old Mr. Boston
    Five Star Brandy
1 dash Bitters
Stir with ice and strain into cocktail glass.

CHARLIE CHAPLIN
1 oz. Old Mr. Boston
    Sloe Gin
1 oz. Old Mr. Boston
    Apricot Flavored Brandy
1 oz. Lemon Juice
Shake with ice and strain into old-fashioned glass over ice cubes.

CHATEAU BRIAND'S RUM COW*
1 oz. Mr. Boston Dark Rum
¼ oz. Meyer's Rum
1 teaspoon sugar
2 dashes Agnostura Bitters
¾ cup milk
Blend and strain.

CHELSEA SIDECAR COCKTAIL
Juice ¼ Lemon
¾ oz. Old Mr. Boston
    Triple Sec
¾ oz. Old Mr. Boston
    Dry Gin
Shake with ice and strain into cocktail glass.

CHERIE
Juice 1 Lime
½ oz. Old Mr. Boston
    Triple Sec
1 oz. Old Mr. Boston Rum
½ oz. Old Mr. Boston Wild
    Cherry Flavored Brandy
Shake with ice and strain into cocktail glass. Add a cherry.

CHERRY BLOSSOM COCKTAIL
1½ oz. Old Mr. Boston
    Five Star Brandy
½ oz. Old Mr. Boston Wild
    Cherry Flavored Brandy
1½ teaspoon Old Mr. Boston
    Triple Sec
1½ teaspoons Grenadine
2 teaspoons Lemon Juice
Shake with ice and strain into cocktail glass with its rim moistened with cherry liqueur and dipped into powdered sugar. Add a Maraschino cherry.

CHERRY COOLER
Pour 2 oz. Old Mr. Boston Cherry Vodka *into collins glass over ice cubes. Fill with cola, add slice of lemon, and stir.*

CHERRY FIZZ
Juice ½ Lemon
2 oz. Old Mr. Boston Wild
    Cherry Flavored Brandy
Shake with ice and strain into highball glass with two cubes of ice. Fill with carbonated water and decorate with a cherry.

CHERRY FLIP
1 Whole Egg
1 teaspoon Powdered Sugar
1½ oz. Old Mr. Boston Wild
    Cherry Flavored Brandy
2 teaspoons Sweet Cream
    (if desired)
Shake with ice and strain into flip glass. Sprinkle a little nutmeg on top.

*Chateau Briand, Dallas, Texas

CHERRY RUM

1¼ oz. Old Mr. Boston Rum
1½ teaspoons Old Mr. Boston
  Wild Cherry Flavored
  Brandy
1 tablespoon Sweet Cream
Shake with ice and strain into cocktail glass.

CHERRY SLING

2 oz. Old Mr. Boston Wild
  Cherry Flavored Brandy
Juice ½ Lemon
Serve in old-fashioned glass with ice cubes and stir. Add a twist of lemon peel.

CHERRY WINE COCKTAIL

¾ oz. Danish Cherry Wine
¾ oz. Old Mr. Boston Vodka
Juice ½ Lime
Shake with ice and strain into cocktail glass.

CHICAGO COCKTAIL

2 oz. Old Mr. Boston
  Five Star Brandy
1 dash Bitters
¼ teaspoon Old Mr. Boston
  Triple Sec
Prepare old-fashioned glass by rubbing slice of lemon around rim and then dip in powdered sugar. Stir above ingredients with ice and strain into prepared glass.

CHICAGO FIZZ

Juice ½ Lemon
1 teaspoon Powdered Sugar
1 Egg White
1 oz. Port
1 oz. Old Mr. Boston Rum
Shake with ice and strain into highball glass over two cubes of ice. Fill with carbonated water and stir.

CHINESE COCKTAIL

1 tablespoon Grenadine
1½ oz. Jamaica Rum
1 dash Bitters
1 teaspoon Maraschino
1 teaspoon Old Mr. Boston
  Triple Sec
Shake with ice and strain into cocktail glass.

CHOCOLATE COCKTAIL

1½ oz. Port
1½ teaspoons Chartreuse
  (Yellow)
1 Egg Yolk
1 teaspoon Powered Sugar
Shake with ice and strain into flip glass.

OLD Mr. BOSTON

CHOCOLATE DAISY

Juice ½ Lemon
½ teaspoon Powdered Sugar
1 teaspoon Raspberry Syrup
 or Grenadine
1½ oz. Old Mr. Boston
 Five Star Brandy
1½ oz. Port
*Shake with ice and strain into
stein or metal cup. Add ice
cubes and decorate with fruit.*

CHOCOLATE FLIP

1 Whole Egg
1 teaspoon Powdered Sugar
¾ oz. Old Mr. Boston
 Sloe Gin
¾ oz. Old Mr. Boston
 Five Star Brandy
2 teaspoons Sweet Cream
 (if desired)
*Shake with ice and strain into
flip glass. Sprinkle a little nutmeg on top.*

CHOCOLATE RUM

1 oz. Old Mr. Boston Rum
½ oz. Old Mr. Boston
 Crème de Cacao
½ oz. Old Mr. Boston
 Crème de Menthe (white)
1 tablespoon Sweet Cream
1 teaspoon 151 Proof Rum
*Shake with ice and strain into
old-fashioned glass over ice
cubes.*

CHOCOLATE SOLDIER COCKTAIL

Juice ½ Lime
¾ oz. Dubonnet
1½ oz. Old Mr. Boston
 Dry Gin
*Shake with ice and strain into
cocktail glass.*

CHRISTMAS YULE EGGNOG

*Beat first the yolks and then,
in a separate bowl, the whites
of 1 dozen eggs. Pour them
together and add:*
1 pinch Baking Soda
6 oz. Old Mr. Boston Rum
2 lbs. Granulated Sugar
*Beat into stiff batter. Then
add:*
1 qt. Milk
1 qt. Sweet Cream
2 qts. Old Thompson
 Blended Whiskey
*Stir. Set in refrigerator over-
night. Before serving, stir
again, and serve in punch
glasses. Sprinkle nutmeg on
top.*

CIDER CUP

4 teaspoons Powdered Sugar
6 oz. Carbonated Water
1 oz. Old Mr. Boston
 Triple Sec
2 oz. Old Mr. Boston
 Five Star Brandy
1 pt. Apple Cider
*Fill large glass pitcher with
ice. Stir in the ingredients and
decorate with as many fruits
as available and a rind of cucumber inserted on each side
of pitcher. Top with small
bunch of mint sprigs. Serve in
claret glasses.*

CIDER EGGNOG

1 Whole Egg
1 teaspoon Powdered Sugar
½ cup Milk

Shake with ice and strain into collins glass. Then fill the glass with sweet cider and stir. Sprinkle nutmeg on top.

CLAMATO COCKTAIL

1½ oz. Old Mr. Boston
  Vodka
1 oz. Clam Juice
3 oz. Tomato Juice

Shake with ice, strain, and serve over ice cubes in large old-fashioned glass.

CLARET COBBLER

Dissolve 1 teaspoon powdered sugar in 2 oz. carbonated water; then add 3 oz. Claret. Fill goblet with ice and stir. Decorate with fruits in season. Serve with straws.

CLARET CUP

4 teaspoons Powdered Sugar
6 oz. Carbonated Water
1 oz. Old Mr. Boston
  Triple Sec
2 oz. Old Mr. Boston
  Five Star Brandy
1 pt. Claret

Fill large glass pitcher with ice. Stir in the ingredients and decorate with as many fruits as available and a rind of cucumber inserted on each side of pitcher. Top with small bunch of mint sprigs. Serve in claret glass.

CLARET PUNCH

Juice 1 dozen Lemons

Add enough powdered sugar to sweeten. Pour over large block of ice in punch bowl and stir well. Then add:

1 cup Old Mr. Boston
  Triple Sec
1 pt. Old Mr. Boston
  Five Star Brandy
3 bottles Claret
1 qt. Carbonated Water
1 pt. Strong Tea (optional)

Stir and decorate with fruits in season. Serve in punch glasses.

CLARIDGE COCKTAIL

¾ oz. Old Mr. Boston
  Dry Gin
¾ oz. Dry Vermouth
1 tablespoon Old Mr. Boston
  Apricot Flavored Brandy
1 tablespoon Old Mr. Boston
  Triple Sec

Stir with ice and strain into cocktail glass.

OLD Mr. BOSTON

CLASSIC COCKTAIL

Juice ¼ Lemon
1½ teaspoons Curaçao
1½ teaspoons Maraschino
1 oz. Old Mr. Boston
    Five Star Brandy
*Prepare rim of old-fashioned
glass by rubbing with lemon
and dipping into powdered
sugar. Shake ingredients with
ice and strain into prepared
glass.*

CLOVE COCKTAIL

1 oz. Sweet Vermouth
½ oz. Old Mr. Boston
    Sloe Gin
½ oz. Muscatel
*Stir with ice and strain into
cocktail glass.*

CLOVER CLUB COCKTAIL

Juice ½ Lemon
2 teaspoons Grenadine
1 Egg White
1½ oz. Old Mr. Boston
    Dry Gin
*Shake with ice and strain into
cocktail glass.*

CLOVER LEAF COCKTAIL

Juice 1 Lime
2 teaspoons Grenadine
1 Egg White
1½ oz. Old Mr. Boston
    Dry Gin
*Shake with ice and strain into
cocktail glass. Serve with mint
leaf on top.*

CLUB COCKTAIL

1½ oz. Old Mr. Boston
    Dry Gin
¾ oz. Sweet Vermouth
*Stir with ice and strain into
cocktail glass. Add a cherry
or olive.*

COBBLERS

*See Index on page 198 for
complete list of Cobbler recipes.*

COCOMACOQUE

Juice ½ Lemon
2 oz. Pineapple Juice
2 oz. Orange Juice
1½ oz. Old Mr. Boston Rum
2 oz. Burgundy
*Shake all ingredients except
wine. Pour into collins glass
over ice cubes and top with
wine. Add pineapple stick.*

COFFEE COCKTAIL

1 Whole Egg
1 teaspoon Powdered Sugar
1 oz. Port
1 oz. Old Mr. Boston
    Five Star Brandy
*Shake with ice and strain into
flip glass. Sprinkle nutmeg on
top.*

COFFEE FLIP

1 Whole Egg
1 teaspoon Powdered Sugar
1 oz. Old Mr. Boston
    Five Star Brandy
1 oz. Port
2 teaspoons Sweet Cream
    (if desired)
*Shake with ice and strain into
flip glass. Sprinkle a little nutmeg on top.*

WRIGHT & GILL
The Quill
STATIONERS

Old Mr. Boston English Market Distilled Dry Gin—80 Proof ▶

COFFEE GRASSHOPPER

¾ oz. Old Mr. Boston
    Coffee Flavored Brandy
¾ oz. Old Mr. Boston
    Crème de Menthe (White)
¾ oz. Sweet Cream
Shake with ice and strain into old-fashioned glass over ice cubes.

COFFEE SOUR

1½ oz. Old Mr. Boston
    Coffee Flavored Brandy
1 oz. Lemon Juice
1 teaspoon Powdered Sugar
½ Egg White
Shake with ice and strain into sour glass.

COGNAC COUPLING

2 oz. Remy Martin Cognac
1 oz. Tawny Port
½ oz. Absinthe Substitute
1 teaspoon Lemon Juice
Shake with ice and strain into old-fashioned glass over ice cubes.

COGNAC HIGHBALL

2 oz. Remy Martin Cognac
Pour into highball glass over ice cubes and fill with ginger ale or carbonated water. Add twist of lemon peel, if desired, and stir.

COLD DECK COCKTAIL

½ teaspoon Old Mr. Boston
    Crème de Menthe (White)
½ oz. Sweet Vermouth
1 oz. Old Mr. Boston
    Five Star Brandy
Stir with ice and strain into cocktail glass.

COLE'S RASPBERRY DREAM*

1½ tablespoons raspberry
    yogurt
1½ tablespoons raspberry
    ice cream
1½ oz. Mr. Boston Crème
    de Cacao (White)
1½ oz. Mr. Boston Vodka
2 oz. heavy cream
Shake or blend.

COLLINS

See Index on page 199 for complete list of Collins recipes.

COLONIAL COCKTAIL

½ oz. Grapefruit Juice
1 teaspoon Maraschino
1½ oz. Old Mr. Boston
    Dry Gin
Shake with ice and strain into cocktail glass. Serve with an olive.

COMBO

2½ oz. Dry Vermouth
1 teaspoon Old Mr. Boston
    Five Star Brandy
½ teaspoon Old Mr. Boston
    Triple Sec
½ teaspoon Powdered Sugar
1 dash Bitters
Shake with ice and strain into old-fashioned glass over ice cubes.

*Cole's Restaurant, Buffalo, N.Y.

COMMODORE COCKTAIL
Juice ½ Lime or ¼ Lemon
1 teaspoon Powdered Sugar
2 dashes Orange Bitters
1½ oz. Old Thompson
    Blended Whiskey
Shake with ice and strain into cocktail glass.

CONTINENTAL
1¾ oz. Old Mr. Boston Rum
1 tablespoon Lime Juice
1½ teaspoons Old Mr. Boston
    Crème de Menthe (Green)
½ teaspoon Powdered Sugar
Shake with ice and strain into cocktail glass. Add twist of lemon peel.

COOLERS
See Index on page 199 for complete list of Cooler recipes.

COOPERSTOWN COCKTAIL
½ oz. Dry Vermouth
½ oz. Sweet Vermouth
1 oz. Old Mr. Boston Dry Gin
Shake with ice and strain into cocktail glass. Add sprig of mint.

CORKSCREW
1½ oz. Old Mr. Boston Rum
½ oz. Dry Vermouth
½ oz. Old Mr. Boston
    Peach Flavored Brandy
Shake with ice and strain into cocktail glass. Garnish with a lime slice.

CORNELL COCKTAIL
½ teaspoon Lemon Juice
1 teaspoon Maraschino
1 Egg White
1½ oz. Old Mr. Boston
    Dry Gin
Shake with ice and strain into cocktail glass.

CORONATION COCKTAIL
¾ oz. Old Mr. Boston
    Dry Gin
¾ oz. Dubonnet
¾ oz. Dry Vermouth
Stir with ice and strain into cocktail glass.

COUNT CURREY
1½ oz. Old Mr. Boston
    Dry Gin
1 teaspoon Powdered Sugar
Shake with ice and strain into champagne glass over ice cubes. Fill with chilled champagne.

OLD Mr. BOSTON

COUNTRY CLUB COOLER

Into collins glass, put ½ teaspoon Grenadine and 2 oz. Carbonated Water and stir. Add ice cubes and 2 oz. Dry Vermouth. Fill with carbonated water or ginger ale and stir again. Insert spiral of orange or lemon peel (or both) and dangle end over rim of glass.

COWBOY COCKTAIL

1½ oz. Old Thompson
    Blended Whiskey
1 tablespoon Sweet Cream
Shake with ice and strain into cocktail glass.

CREAM FIZZ

Juice ½ Lemon
1 teaspoon Powdered Sugar
2 oz. Old Mr. Boston Dry Gin
1 teaspoon Sweet Cream
Shake with ice and strain into highball glass over two cubes of ice. Fill with carbonated water and stir.

CREAM PUFF

2 oz. Old Mr. Boston Rum
1 oz. Sweet Cream
½ teaspoon Powdered Sugar
Shake with ice and strain into highball glass over two cubes of ice. Fill with carbonated water and stir.

CREAMY ORANGE

1 oz. Orange Juice
1 oz. Cream Sherry
¾ oz. Old Mr. Boston
    Five Star Brandy
1 tablespoon Sweet Cream
Shake with ice and strain into cocktail glass.

CREAMY SCREWDRIVER

2 oz. Old Mr. Boston Vodka
1 Egg Yolk
6 oz. Orange Juice
1 teaspoon Sugar
Combine all ingredients with half a cup of crushed ice in a blender. Blend at low speed and pour into collins glass with ice cubes.

CRÈME DE CAFÉ

1 oz. Old Mr. Boston
    Coffee Flavored Brandy
½ oz. Old Mr. Boston Rum
½ oz. Old Mr. Boston
    Anisette
1 oz. Sweet Cream
Shake with ice and strain into old-fashioned glass over ice cubes.

CRÈME DE GIN COCKTAIL

1½ oz. Old Mr. Boston
    Dry Gin
½ oz. Old Mr. Boston
    Crème de Menthe (White)
1 Egg White
2 teaspoons Lemon Juice
2 teaspoons Orange Juice
Shake with ice and strain into cocktail glass.

CRÈME DE MENTHE FRAPPÉ

Fill cocktail glass up to brim with shaved ice. Add Old Mr. Boston Crème de Menthe (Green). Serve with two short straws.

CREOLE

1½ oz. Old Mr. Boston Rum
1 dash Tabasco Sauce
1 teaspoon Lemon Juice
Salt and Pepper
Shake with ice and strain into old-fashioned glass over ice cubes. Fill with cold beef bouillon and stir.

CREOLE LADY COCKTAIL

1½ oz. Old Kentucky Tavern
   Bourbon Whiskey
1½ oz. Madeira
1 teaspoon Grenadine
Stir with ice and strain into cocktail glass. Serve with one green and one red cherry.

CRIMSON COCKTAIL

1½ oz. Old Mr. Boston
   Dry Gin
2 teaspoons Lemon Juice
1 teaspoon Grenadine
Shake with ice and strain into cocktail glass, leaving enough room on top to float ¾ oz. Port.

CRYSTAL SLIPPER COCKTAIL

½ oz. Blue Curacao
2 dashes Orange Bitters
1½ oz. Old Mr. Boston
   Dry Gin
Stir with ice and strain into cocktail glass.

CUBA LIBRE

Put juice ½ lime and rind in glass. Add 2 oz. Old Mr. Boston Rum. Fill highball glass with cola and ice cubes.

CUBAN COCKTAIL NO. 1

Juice ½ Lime
½ teaspoon Powdered Sugar
2 oz. Old Mr. Boston Rum
Shake with ice and strain into cocktail glass.

CUBAN COCKTAIL NO. 2

Juice ½ Lime or ¼ Lemon
½ oz. Old Mr. Boston
   Apricot Flavored Brandy
1½ oz. Old Mr. Boston
   Five Star Brandy
1 teaspoon Old Mr. Boston
   Rum
Shake with ice and strain into cocktail glass.

CUBAN SPECIAL COCKTAIL

1 tablespoon Pineapple Juice
Juice ½ Lime
1 oz. Old Mr. Boston Rum
½ teaspoon Old Mr. Boston
   Triple Sec
Shake with ice and strain into cocktail glass. Decorate with stick of pineapple and a cherry.

CUPS

See Index on page 200 for complete list of Cup recipes.

D

DAIQUIRI COCKTAIL
Juice 1 Lime
1 teaspoon Powdered Sugar
1½ oz. Old Mr. Boston Rum
Shake with ice and strain into cocktail glass.

DAISIES
See Index on page 201 for complete list of Daisy recipes.

DAMN-THE-WEATHER COCKTAIL
1 teaspoon Old Mr. Boston Triple Sec
1 tablespoon Orange Juice
1 tablespoon Sweet Vermouth
1 oz. Old Mr. Boston Dry Gin
Shake with ice and strain into cocktail glass.

DARB COCKTAIL
1 teaspoon Lemon Juice
¾ oz. Dry Vermouth
¾ oz. Old Mr. Boston Dry Gin
¾ oz. Old Mr. Boston Apricot Flavored Brandy
Shake with ice and strain into cocktail glass.

DEAUVILLE COCKTAIL
Juice ¼ Lemon
½ oz. Old Mr. Boston Five Star Brandy
½ oz. Apple Brandy
½ oz. Old Mr. Boston Triple Sec
Shake with ice and strain into cocktail glass.

DEEP SEA COCKTAIL
1 oz. Dry Vermouth
¼ teaspoon Absinthe Substitute
1 dash Orange Bitters
1 oz. Old Mr. Boston Dry Gin
Stir with ice and strain into cocktail glass.

DELMONICO NO. 1
¾ oz. Old Mr. Boston Dry Gin
½ oz. Dry Vermouth
½ oz. Sweet Vermouth
½ oz. Old Mr. Boston Five Star Brandy
Stir with ice and strain into cocktail glass. Add a twist of lemon peel.

DELMONICO NO. 2
1 dash Orange Bitters
1 oz. Dry Vermouth
1½ oz. Old Mr. Boston Dry Gin
Stir with ice and strain into cocktail glass. Add twist of lemon peel.

DEMPSEY COCKTAIL

1 oz. Old Mr. Boston Dry Gin
1 oz. Apple Brandy
½ teaspoon Absinthe
    Substitute
½ teaspoon Grenadine
Stir wih ice and strain into cocktail glass.

DEPTH BOMB

1 oz. Apple Brandy
1 oz. Old Mr. Boston
    Five Star Brandy
1 dash Lemon Juice
1 dash Grenadine
Shake with ice and strain into old-fashioned glass over ice cubes.

DERBY DAIQUIRI

1½ oz. Old Mr. Boston Rum
1 oz. Orange Juice
1 tablespoon Lime Juice
1 teaspoon Sugar
Combine all ingredients with half a cup of shaved ice in a blender. Blend at low speed. Pour into champagne glass.

DERBY FIZZ

Juice ½ Lemon
1 teaspoon Powdered Sugar
1 Whole Egg
2 oz. Desmond & Duff
    Scotch Whisky
1 teaspoon Old Mr. Boston
    Triple Sec
Shake with ice and strain into highball glass over two ice cubes. Fill with carbonated water and stir.

DEVIL'S COCKTAIL

½ teaspoon Lemon Juice
1½ oz. Port
1½ oz. Dry Vermouth
Stir with ice and strain into cocktail glass.

DEVIL'S TAIL

1½ oz. Old Mr. Boston Rum
1 oz. Old Mr. Boston Vodka
1 tablespoon Lime Juice
1½ teaspoons Grenadine
1½ teaspoons Old Mr. Boston
    Apricot Flavored Brandy
Combine all ingredients with half cup of crushed ice in a blender. Blend at low speed and pour into champagne glass. Add twist of lime peel.

DIAMOND FIZZ
Juice ½ Lemon
1 teaspoon Powdered Sugar
2 oz. Old Mr. Boston Dry Gin
Shake with ice and strain into highball glass over two cubes of ice. Fill with champagne and stir.

DIANA COCKTAIL
Fill cocktail glass with ice, then fill ¾ full with Old Mr. Boston Crème de Menthe (White) *and float* Old Mr. Boston Five Star Brandy *on top.*

DILLATINI COCKTAIL
See Special Martini Section on pages 173 and 174.

DINAH COCKTAIL
Juice ¼ Lemon
½ teaspoon Powdered Sugar
1½ oz. Old Thompson Blended Whiskey
Shake well with ice and strain into cocktail glass. Serve with a mint leaf.

DIPLOMAT COCKTAIL
1½ oz. Dry Vermouth
½ oz. Sweet Vermouth
2 dashes Bitters
½ teaspoon Maraschino
Stir with ice and strain into cocktail glass. Serve with a half slice of lemon and a cherry.

DIXIE COCKTAIL
Juice ¼ Orange
1 tablespoon Absinthe Substitute
½ oz. Dry Vermouth
1 oz. Old Mr. Boston Dry Gin
Shake with ice and strain into cocktail glass.

DIXIE JULEP
Into a collins glass put:
1 teaspoon Powdered Sugar
2½ oz. Old Kentucky Tavern Bourbon Whiskey
Fill with ice and stir gently until glass is frosted. Decorate with sprigs of mint. Serve with straws.

DIXIE WHISKEY COCKTAIL
½ teaspoon Powdered Sugar
1 dash Bitters
¼ teaspoon Old Mr. Boston Triple Sec
½ teaspoon Old Mr. Boston Crème de Menthe (White)
2 oz. Old Kentucky Tavern Bourbon Whiskey
Shake with ice and strain into cocktail glass.

DOUBLE STANDARD SOUR
Juice ½ Lemon or 1 Lime
½ teaspoon Powdered Sugar
¾ oz. Old Thompson Blended Whiskey
¾ oz. Old Mr. Boston Dry Gin
½ teaspoon Raspberry Syrup or Grenadine
Shake with ice and strain into sour glass. Decorate with a half slice of lemon and a cherry.

DR. COOK

¾ oz. Old Mr. Boston
    Dry Gin
1 tablespoon Lemon Juice
1 dash Maraschino
1 Egg White
Shake with ice and strain into wine glass.

DREAM COCKTAIL

¾ oz. Old Mr. Boston
    Triple Sec
1½ oz. Old Mr. Boston
    Five Star Brandy
¼ teaspoon Old Mr. Boston
    Anisette
Shake with ice and strain into cocktail glass.

DRY MARTINI COCKTAIL

See Special Martini Section on pages 173 and 174

DU BARRY COCKTAIL

1 dash Bitters
¾ oz. Dry Vermouth
½ teaspoon Absinthe
    Substitute
1½ oz. Old Mr. Boston
    Dry Gin
Stir with ice and strain into cocktail glass. Add slice of orange.

DUBONNET COCKTAIL

1½ oz. Dubonnet
¾ oz. Old Mr. Boston
    Dry Gin
1 dash Orange Bitters
    (if desired)
Stir with ice and strain into cocktail glass. Add a twist of lemon peel.

DUBONNET FIZZ

Juice ½ Orange
Juice ¼ Lemon
1 teaspoon Old Mr. Boston
    Wild Cherry Flavored
    Brandy
2 oz. Dubonnet
Shake with ice and strain into highball glass over two cubes of ice. Fill with carbonated water and stir.

DUBONNET HIGHBALL

Put 2 oz. Dubonnet in highball glass with two cubes of ice and fill with ginger ale or carbonated water. Add twist of lemon peel, if desired, and stir.

DUCHESS

1½ oz. Absinthe Substitute
½ oz. Dry Vermouth
½ oz. Sweet Vermouth
Shake with ice and strain into cocktail glass.

DUKE COCKTAIL

½ oz. Old Mr. Boston
    Triple Sec
1 teaspoon Orange Juice
2 teaspoons Lemon Juice
½ teaspoon Maraschino
1 Whole Egg
Shake with ice and strain into stem glass. Fill with chilled champagne and stir.

E

East India Cocktail No. 1

1½ oz. Old Mr. Boston
  Five Star Brandy
½ teaspoon Pineapple Juice
½ teaspoon Old Mr. Boston
  Triple Sec
1 teaspoon Jamaica Rum
1 dash Bitters
Shake with ice and strain into cocktail glass. Add a twist of lemon peel and a cherry.

East India Cocktail No. 2

1½ oz. Dry Vermouth
1½ oz. Dry Sherry
1 dash Orange Bitters
Stir with ice and strain into cocktail glass.

Eclipse Cocktail

1 oz. Old Mr. Boston Dry Gin
2 oz. Old Mr. Boston Sloe Gin
½ teaspoon Lemon Juice
Put enough grenadine into cocktail glass to cover a ripe olive. Mix the above ingredients in ice and pour onto the grenadine so that they do not mix.

Eggnogs

See Index on page 204 for complete list of Eggnog recipes.

Egg Sour

1 Whole Egg
1 teaspoon Powdered Sugar
Juice ½ Lemon
2 oz. Old Mr. Boston
  Five Star Brandy
¼ teaspoon Old Mr. Boston
  Triple Sec
Shake with ice and strain into old-fashioned glass.

El Presidente Cocktail No. 1

Juice 1 Lime
1 teaspoon Pineapple Juice
1 teaspoon Grenadine
1½ oz. Old Mr. Boston Rum
Shake with ice and strain into cocktail glass.

El Presidente Cocktail No. 2

¾ oz. Dry Vermouth
1½ oz. Old Mr. Boston Rum
1 dash Bitters
Stir with ice and strain into cocktail glass.

ELK'S OWN COCKTAIL

1 Egg White
1½ oz. Old Thompson
    Blended Whiskey
¾ oz. Port
Juice ¼ Lemon
1 teaspoon Powdered Sugar
Shake with ice and strain into cocktail glass. Add a strip of pineapple.

EMERALD ISLE COCKTAIL

2 oz. Old Mr. Boston Dry Gin
1 teaspoon Old Mr. Boston
    Crème de Menthe (Green)
3 dashes Bitters
Stir with ice and strain into cocktail glass.

EMERSON

1½ oz. Old Mr. Boston
    Dry Gin
1 oz. Sweet Vermouth
Juice ½ Lime
1 teaspoon Maraschino
Shake with ice and strain into cocktail glass.

ENGLISH COFFEE

Greensleeves Mint Cream
    Liqueur
Coffee
½ pint whipping cream
Whip cream to a thick consistency and fold in ½ cup Greensleeves. To a cup of hot coffee, add 1 ounce of Greensleeves. Top with the Greensleeves and whipped cream mixture.
Topping makes 6-8 servings.
Note: If desired, several drops of green food coloring may be added.

ENGLISH HIGHBALL

¾ oz. Old Mr. Boston
    Dry Gin
¾ oz. Old Mr. Boston
    Five Star Brandy
¾ oz. Sweet Vermouth
Pour into highball glass over ice cubes and fill with ginger ale or carbonated water. Add twist of lemon peel, if desired, and stir.

ENGLISH ROSE COCKTAIL

1½ oz. Old Mr. Boston
    Dry Gin
¾ oz. Old Mr. Boston
    Apricot Flavored Brandy
¾ oz. Dry Vermouth
1 teaspoon Grenadine
¼ teaspoon Lemon Juice
Prepare rim of glass by rubbing with lemon and dipping in sugar. Shake with ice and strain into cocktail glass. Serve with a cherry.

ETHEL DUFFY COCKTAIL

¾ oz. Old Mr. Boston
    Apricot Flavored Brandy
¾ oz. Old Mr. Boston
    Crème de Menthe (White)
¾ oz. Old Mr. Boston Triple
    Sec
Shake with ice and strain into cocktail glass.

EVERYBODY'S IRISH COCKTAIL

1 teaspoon Old Mr. Boston
    Crème de Menthe (Green)
1 teaspoon Chartreuse
    (Green)
2 oz. Irish Whisky

Stir with ice and strain into cocktail glass. Serve with green olive.

EYE-OPENER COCKTAIL

1 Egg Yolk
½ Teaspoon Powdered Sugar
1 teaspoon Absinthe
    Substitute
1 teaspoon Old Mr. Boston
    Triple Sec
1 teaspoon Old Mr. Boston
    Crème de Cacao (White)
2 oz. Old Mr. Boston Rum

Shake with ice and strain into flip glass.

F

FAIR-AND-WARMER COCKTAIL
¾ oz. Sweet Vermouth
1½ oz. Old Mr. Boston Rum
½ teaspoon Old Mr. Boston Triple Sec
Stir with ice and strain into cocktail glass.

FAIRY BELLE COCKTAIL
1 Egg White
1 teaspoon Grenadine
¾ oz. Old Mr. Boston Apricot Flavored Brandy
1½ oz. Old Mr. Boston Dry Gin
Shake with ice and strain into cocktail glass.

FALLEN ANGEL COCKTAIL
Juice 1 Lime or ½ Lemon
1½ oz. Old Mr. Boston Dry Gin
1 dash Bitters
½ teaspoon Old Mr. Boston Crème de Menthe (White)
Shake with ice and strain into cocktail glass. Serve with a cherry.

FANCY BRANDY COCKTAIL
2 oz. Old Mr. Boston Five Star Brandy
1 dash Bitters
¼ teaspoon Old Mr. Boston Triple Sec
¼ teaspoon Powdered Sugar
Shake with ice and strain into cocktail glass. Add a twist of lemon peel.

FANCY GIN COCKTAIL
Same as Fancy Brandy Cocktail but made with 2 oz. Old Mr. Boston Dry Gin.

FANCY WHISKEY COCKTAIL
Same as Fancy Brandy Cocktail except made with 2 oz. Old Thompson Blended Whiskey.

FANTASIO COCKTAIL
1 teaspoon Old Mr. Boston Crème de Menthe (White)
1 teaspoon Maraschino
1 oz. Old Mr. Boston Five Star Brandy
¾ oz. Dry Vermouth
Stir with ice and strain into cocktail glass.

FARE THEE WELL

1½ oz. Old Mr. Boston
    Dry Gin
½ oz. Dry Vermouth
1 dash Sweet Vermouth
1 dash Old Mr. Boston Triple
    Sec
Shake with ice and strain into cocktail glass.

FARMER'S COCKTAIL

1 oz. Old Mr. Boston Dry Gin
½ oz. Dry Vermouth
½ oz. Sweet Vermouth
2 dashes Bitters
Stir with ice and strain into cocktail glass.

FAVORITE COCKTAIL

¾ oz. Old Mr. Boston
    Apricot Flavored Brandy
¾ oz. Dry Vermouth
¾ oz. Old Mr. Boston
    Dry Gin
¼ teaspoon Lemon Juice
Shake with ice and strain into cocktail glass.

FIFTH AVENUE

½ oz. Old Mr. Boston
    Crème de Cacao
½ oz. Old Mr. Boston
    Apricot Flavored Brandy
1 tablespoon Sweet Cream
Pour carefully, in order given, into parfait glass, so that each ingredient floats on preceding one.

FIFTY-FIFTY COCKTAIL

1½ oz. Old Mr. Boston
    Dry Gin
1½ oz. Dry Vermouth
Stir with ice and strain into cocktail glass.

FINE-AND-DANDY COCKTAIL

Juice ¼ Lemon
½ oz. Old Mr. Boston
    Triple Sec
1½ oz. Old Mr. Boston
    Dry Gin
1 dash Bitters
Shake with ice and strain into cocktail glass. Serve with a cherry.

FINO MARTINI

2 oz. Old Mr. Boston Dry Gin
2 teaspoons Fino Sherry
Stir with ice and strain into cocktail glass. Add twist of lemon peel.

FIREMAN'S SOUR

Juice 2 Limes
½ teaspoon Powdered Sugar
1 tablespoon Grenadine
2 oz. Old Mr. Boston Rum
Shake with ice and strain into delmonico glass. Fill with carbonated water, if desired. Decorate with a half slice of lemon and a cherry.

FISH HOUSE PUNCH

Juice 1 dozen Lemons.
Add enough powdered sugar to sweeten. Pour over large block of ice in punch bowl and stir well. Then add:
1½ qts. Old Mr. Boston
    Five Star Brandy
1 pt. Old Mr. Boston
    Peach Flavored Brandy
1 pt. Old Mr. Boston Rum
1 qt. Carbonated Water
1 pt. Strong Tea (optional)
Stir well and decorate with fruits in season. Serve in punch glasses.

OLD Mr. BOSTON

FIXES
See Index on page 204 for complete list of Fix recipes.

FIZZES
See Index on page 204 for complete list of Fizz recipes.

FLAMINGO COCKTAIL
Juice ½ Lime
½ oz. Old Mr. Boston Apricot Flavored Brandy
1½ oz. Old Mr. Boston Dry Gin
1 teaspoon Grenadine
Shake with ice and strain into cocktail glass.

FLIPS
See Index on page 205 for complete list of Flip recipes.

FLORADORA COOLER
Into collins glass put:
Juice 1 Lime
½ teaspoon Powdered Sugar
1 tablespoon Raspberry Syrup or Grenadine
2 oz. Carbonated Water
Stir. Fill glass with ice and add 2 oz. Old Mr. Boston Dry Gin. Fill with carbonated water or ginger ale and stir again.

FLORIDA
½ oz. Old Mr. Boston Dry Gin
1½ teaspoons Kirschwasser
1½ teaspoons Old Mr. Boston Triple Sec
1 oz. Orange Juice
1 teaspoon Lemon Juice
Shake with ice and strain into cocktail glass.

FLYING DUTCHMAN
2 oz. Old Mr. Boston Dry Gin
1 dash Old Mr. Boston Triple Sec
Shake with ice and strain into old-fashioned glass over ice cubes.

FLYING GRASSHOPPER COCKTAIL
¾ oz. Old Mr. Boston Crème de Menthe (Green)
¾ oz. Old Mr. Boston Crème de Cacao (White)
¾ oz. Old Mr. Boston Vodka
Stir with ice and strain into cocktail glass.

FLYING SCOTCHMAN COCKTAIL
1 oz. Sweet Vermouth
1 oz. Desmond & Duff Scotch Whisky
1 dash Bitters
¼ teaspoon Sugar Syrup
Stir with ice and strain into cocktail glass.

FOG CUTTER

1½ oz. Old Mr. Boston Rum
½ oz. Old Mr. Boston
   Five Star Brandy
½ oz. Old Mr. Boston
   Dry Gin
1 oz. Orange Juice
1½ oz. Lemon Juice
1½ teaspoons Orgeat Syrup
Shake all ingredients and strain into collins glass over ice cubes. Top with a teaspoon of sweet sherry.

FOG HORN

Juice ½ Lime
1½ oz. Old Mr. Boston
   Dry Gin
Pour into highball glass over ice cubes. Fill with ginger ale. Stir. Add a piece of lime.

FONTAINEBLEAU SPECIAL

1 oz. Old Mr. Boston
   Five Star Brandy
1 oz. Old Mr. Boston Anisette
½ oz. Dry Vermouth
Shake with ice and strain into cocktail glass.

FORT LAUDERDALE

1½ oz. Old Mr. Boston Rum
½ oz. Sweet Vermouth
Juice ¼ Orange
Juice ¼ Lime
Shake with ice and strain into old-fashioned glass over ice cubes. Add slice of orange.

FOX RIVER COCKTAIL

1 tablespoon Old Mr. Boston
   Crème de Cacao
2 oz. Old Thompson
   Blended Whiskey
4 dashes Bitters
Stir with ice and strain into cocktail glass.

FRANKENJACK COCKTAIL

1 oz. Old Mr. Boston Dry Gin
¾ oz. Dry Vermouth
½ oz. Old Mr. Boston
   Apricot Flavored Brandy
1 teaspoon Old Mr. Boston
   Triple Sec
Stir with ice and strain into cocktail glass. Serve with a cherry.

OLD Mr. BOSTON

FREE SILVER
Juice ¼ Lemon
½ teaspoon Powdered Sugar
1½ oz. Old Mr. Boston
    Dry Gin
½ oz. Old Mr. Boston
    Dark Rum
1 tablespoon Milk
Shake with ice and strain into collins glass over ice cubes. Add carbonated water.

FRENCH CONNECTION
1½ oz. Remy Martin Cognac
¾ oz. Amaretto di Saronno
Serve in an old-fashioned glass over ice.

FRENCH "75"
Juice 1 Lemon
2 teaspoons Powdered Sugar
Stir in collins glass. Then add cubes of ice, 2 oz. Old Mr. Boston Dry Gin; fill with champagne and stir. Decorate with slice of lemon or orange and a cherry. Serve with straws.

FRISCO SOUR
Juice ¼ Lemon
Juice ½ Lime
½ oz. Benedictine
2 oz. Old Thompson
    Blended Whiskey
Shake with ice and strain into sour glass. Decorate with slices of lemon and lime.

FROTH BLOWER COCKTAIL
1 Egg White
1 teaspoon Grenadine
2 oz. Old Mr. Boston Dry Gin
Shake with ice and strain into cocktail glass.

FROUPE COCKTAIL
1½ oz. Sweet Vermouth
1½ oz. Old Mr. Boston
    Five Star Brandy
1 teaspoon Benedictine
Stir with ice and strain into cocktail glass.

FROZEN APPLE
1½ oz. Applejack
1 tablespoon Lime Juice
1 teaspoon Sugar
½ Egg White
Combine ingredients with a cup of crushed ice in a blender and blend at low speed. Pour into old-fashioned glass.

FROZEN BERKELEY
1½ oz. Old Mr. Boston Rum
½ oz. Old Mr. Boston
    Five Star Brandy
1 tablespoon Passion Fruit
    Syrup
1 tablespoon Lemon Juice
Combine ingredients with half a cup of crushed ice in a blender and blend at low speed. Pour into champagne glass.

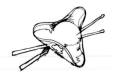

FROZEN BRANDY AND RUM

1½ oz. Old Mr. Boston
    Five Star Brandy
1 oz. Old Mr. Boston Rum
1 tablespoon Lemon Juice
1 Egg Yolk
1 teaspoon Powdered Sugar
Combine ingredients with a cup of crushed ice in a blender and blend at low speed. Pour into old-fashioned glass.

FROZEN DAIQUIRI

1½ oz. Old Mr. Boston Rum
1 tablespoon Old Mr. Boston
    Triple Sec
1½ oz. Lime Juice
1 teaspoon Sugar
1 cup Crushed Ice
Combine ingredients in a blender and blend at low speed for five seconds. Then blend at high speed until firm. Pour into champagne glass. Top with a cherry.

FROZEN MATADOR

1½ oz. Gavilan Tequila
2 oz. Pineapple Juice
1 tablespoon Lime Juice
Combine all ingredients with a cup of crushed ice in blender. Blend at low speed and pour into old-fashioned glass. Add pineapple stick.

FROZEN MINT DAIQUIRI

2 oz. Old Mr. Boston Rum
1 tablespoon Lime Juice
6 Mint Leaves
1 teaspoon Sugar
Combine all ingredients with a cup of crushed ice in blender, and blend at low speed. Pour into old-fashioned glass.

FROZEN PINEAPPLE DAIQUIRI

1½ oz. Old Mr. Boston Rum
4 Pineapple Chunks
    (Canned)
1 tablespoon Lime Juice
½ teaspoon Sugar
Combine all ingredients with a cup of crushed ice in blender. Blend at low speed and pour into champagne glass.

GABLES COLLINS

1½ oz. Mr. Boston Vodka
1 oz. Mr. Boston
    Crème de Noyaux
1 tablespoon Lemon Juice
1 tablespoon Pineapple Juice
Shake with ice and strain into collins glass over ice cubes. Add carbonated water. Decorate with slice of lemon and a pineapple chunk.

GAUGUIN

2 oz. Old Mr. Boston Rum
1 tablespoon Passion Fruit
    Syrup
1 tablespoon Lemon Juice
1 tablespoon Lime Juice
Combine ingredients with a cup of crushed ice in a blender and blend at low speed. Serve in an old-fashioned glass. Top with a cherry.

GENERAL HARRISON'S EGGNOG

1 Whole Egg
1 teaspoon Powdered Sugar
Shake with ice and strain into collins glass. Fill glass with claret or sweet cider and stir. Sprinkle nutmeg on top.

GENTLE BEN

1 oz. Old Mr. Boston
    Vodka
1 oz. Old Mr. Boston
    Dry Gin
1 oz. Gavilan Tequila
Shake all ingredients with ice and pour into collins glass over ice cubes. Fill with orange juice and stir. Decorate with orange slice and a cherry.

GEORGIA MINT JULEP

2 Sprigs Mint Leaves
1 teaspoon Powdered Sugar
1½ oz. Old Mr. Boston
    Five Star Brandy
1 oz. Old Mr. Boston
    Peach Flavored Brandy
Place mint leaves in collins glass with ice. Add teaspoon sugar and a little water. Muddle and fill with brandy and peach liqueur. Decorate with mint leaves.

GIBSON COCKTAIL

See Special Martini Section on pages 173 and 174

GILROY COCKTAIL

Juice ¼ Lemon
1 tablespoon Dry Vermouth
¾ oz. Old Mr. Boston Wild
    Cherry Flavored Brandy
¾ oz. Old Mr. Boston
    Dry Gin
1 dash Orange Bitters
Shake with ice and strain into cocktail glass.

GIMLET COCKTAIL

1 oz. Rose's Lime Juice
1 teaspoon Powdered Sugar
1½ oz. Old Mr. Boston
    Dry Gin
Shake with ice and strain into cocktail glass.

GIN ALOHA

1½ oz. Old Mr. Boston
    Dry Gin
1½ teaspoon Old Mr. Boston
    Triple Sec
1 tablespoon Unsweetened
    Pineapple Juice
1 dash Orange Bitters
Shake with ice and strain into cocktail glass.

GIN AND BITTERS

Put ½ teaspoon bitters into cocktail glass and revolve glass until it is entirely coated with the bitters. Then fill with Old Mr. Boston Dry Gin. No ice is used in this drink.

GIN AND IT

2 oz. Old Mr. Boston Dry Gin
1 oz. Sweet Vermouth
Stir ingredients in cocktail glass. No ice is used in this drink.

GIN AND SIN

1 oz. Old Mr. Boston Dry Gin
1 oz. Lemon Juice
1 tablespoon Orange Juice
1 dash Grenadine
Shake with ice and strain into cocktail glass.

GIN AND TONIC

Pour into highball glass 2 oz. Old Mr. Boston Dry Gin over ice cubes and fill with quinine water. Stir.

GIN BUCK

Juice ½ Lemon
1½ oz. Old Mr. Boston
    Dry Gin
Pour ingredients into glass over ice cubes and fill with ginger ale. Stir.

GIN COBBLER

Dissolve 1 teaspoon powdered sugar in 2 oz. carbonated water, then fill goblet with ice and add 2 oz. Old Mr. Boston Dry Gin. Stir and decorate with fruits in season. Serve with straws.

GIN COCKTAIL

2 oz. Old Mr. Boston Dry Gin
2 dashes Bitters
Stir with ice and strain into cocktail glass. Serve with a twist of lemon peel.

GIN COOLER

Into a collins glass, stir ½ teaspoon powdered sugar and 2 oz. carbonated water. Fill glass with ice and add 2 oz. Old Mr. Boston Dry Gin. Fill with carbonated water or ginger ale and stir again. Insert spiral of orange or lemon peel (or both) and dangle end over rim of glass.

GIN DAISY

Juice ½ Lemon
½ teaspoon Powdered Sugar
1 teaspoon Raspberry Syrup
    or Grenadine
2 oz. Old Mr. Boston Dry Gin
Shake with ice and strain into stein or metal cup. Add ice cubes and decorate with fruit.

GIN FIX

Mix juice of half a lemon, 1 teaspoon powdered sugar, and 1 teaspoon water in a highball glass. Stir and fill glass with ice. Add 2½ oz. Old Mr. Boston Dry Gin. Stir, add slice of lemon. Serve with straws.

GIN FIZZ

Juice ½ Lemon
1 teaspoon Powdered Sugar
2 oz. Old Mr. Boston Dry Gin
Shake with ice and strain into highball glass with two ice cubes. Fill with carbonated water and stir.

GIN HIGHBALL

2 oz. Old Mr. Boston Dry Gin
Pour into highball glass over ice cubes and fill with ginger ale or carbonated water. Add twist of lemon peel, if desired, and stir.

GIN MILK PUNCH

1 teaspoon Powdered Sugar
2 oz. Old Mr. Boston Dry Gin
1 cup Milk
Shake with ice, strain into collins glass, and sprinkle nutmeg on top.

GIN RICKEY

Juice ½ Lime
1½ oz. Old Mr. Boston
    Dry Gin
Pour ingredients into highball glass over ice cubes and fill with carbonated water. Stir. Add a wedge of lime.

OLD Mr. BOSTON

GIN SANGAREE

Dissolve ½ teaspoon powdered sugar in one teaspoon of water, and add 2 oz. Old Mr. Boston Dry Gin. *Pour into highball glass over ice cubes. Fill with carbonated water and stir. Float on top a tablespoon of Port. Sprinkle lightly with nutmeg.*

GIN SLING

Dissolve 1 teaspoon powdered sugar in 1 teaspoon water and juice ½ lemon. Add 2 oz. Old Mr. Boston Dry Gin. *Pour into old-fashioned glass over ice cubes and stir. Add a twist of orange peel.*

GIN SMASH

Muddle one lump of sugar with 1 oz. carbonated water and 4 sprigs of mint, and add 2 oz. Old Mr. Boston Dry Gin *and an ice cube. Stir in an old-fashioned glass and decorate with a slice of orange and a cherry. Add a twist of lemon peel.*

GIN SOUR

Juice ½ Lemon
½ teaspoon Powdered Sugar
2 oz. Old Mr. Boston Dry Gin
Shake with ice and strain into sour glass. Decorate with a half-slice of lemon and a cherry.

GIN SQUIRT

1½ oz. Old Mr. Boston Dry Gin
1 tablespoon Powdered Sugar
1 teaspoon Raspberry Syrup or Grenadine
Stir with ice and strain into highball glass over ice cubes. Fill with carbonated water and stir. Decorate with cubes of pineapple and strawberries.

GIN SWIZZLE

Into collins glass put:
Juice 1 Lime
1 teaspoon Powdered Sugar
2 oz. Carbonated Water
Fill glass with ice and stir with swizzle stick. Then add:
2 dashes Bitters
2 oz. Old Mr. Boston Dry Gin
Fill with carbonated water and serve with swizzle stick in glass, allowing individual to do final stirring.

GIN THING

1½ oz. Old Mr. Boston Dry Gin
Juice ½ Lime
Pour gin and lime juice in highball glass over ice cubes and fill with ginger ale.

Toison de Oro Brandy—80 Proof ▶

BRANDY
TOISON
DE
ORO

SOLERA RESERVA

OLD Mr. BOSTON

GIN TODDY

In old-fashioned cocktail glass, mix ½ teaspoon powdered sugar and 2 teaspoons water. Add 2 oz. Old Mr. Boston Dry Gin and an ice cube. Stir and add a twist of lemon peel.

GIN TODDY (HOT)

Put lump of sugar into hot whiskey glass and fill two-thirds with boiling water. Add 2 oz. Old Mr. Boston Dry Gin. Stir and decorate with slice of lemon. Sprinkle nutmeg on top.

GLÖGG

Pour the following into kettle:
2 bottles Wine (Port, Sherry, Claret, Burgundy, or Madeira)
Insert cheesecloth bag containing:
2 oz. Dried Orange Peel
2 oz. Cinnamon Sticks
20 Cardamom Seeds
25 Cloves
and boil slowly for 15 minutes, stirring occasionally. Add 1 lb. each blanched almonds and seedless raisins and continue to boil for additional 15 minutes. Remove kettle from stove and place wire grill containing 1 lb. lump sugar over opening. Pour one fifth of Old Mr. Boston Five Star Brandy over sugar making sure to saturate all of it. Then light sugar with match and let it flame. After sugar has melted replace kettle cover to extinguish flame. Stir again and remove spice bag. Serve hot in punch cups with a few almonds and raisins.

GLOOM LIFTER

1 oz. Old Thompson Blended Whiskey
½ oz. Old Mr. Boston Five Star Brandy
Juice ½ Lemon
1 tablespoon Raspberry Syrup
½ teaspoon Sugar
½ Egg White
Shake with ice and strain into highball glass with ice cubes.

GODFATHER

1½ oz. Desmond & Duff Scotch Whisky
¾ oz. Amaretto di Saronno
Serve in an old-fashioned glass over ice. (Kentucky Tavern Bourbon may also be used.)

GODMOTHER

1½ oz. Mr. Boston Vodka
¾ oz. Amaretto di Saronno
Serve in an old-fashioned glass over ice.

GOLDEN CADILLAC

1 oz. Galliano
2 oz. Old Mr. Boston
    Crème de Cacao (White)
1 oz. Sweet Cream
Combine with half cup of crushed ice in blender at low speed for ten seconds. Strain into champagne glass.

GOLDEN DAWN

1 oz. Apple Brandy
½ oz. Old Mr. Boston
    Apricot Flavored Brandy
½ oz. Old Mr. Boston
    Dry Gin
1 oz. Orange Juice
Shake with ice and strain into old-fashioned glass with cubed ice. Add 1 teaspoon grenadine.

GOLDEN DAZE

1½ oz. Old Mr. Boston Dry
    Gin
½ oz. Old Mr. Boston
    Peach Flavored Brandy
1 oz. Orange Juice
Shake with ice and strain into cocktail glass.

GOLDEN DREAM

1 tablespoon Orange Juice
½ oz. Old Mr. Boston
    Triple Sec
1 oz. Galliano
1 tablespoon Sweet Cream
Shake with ice and strain into cocktail glass.

GOLDEN FIZZ

Juice ½ Lemon
½ tablespoon Powdered Sugar
1½ oz. Old Mr. Boston Dry
    Gin
1 Egg Yolk
Shake with ice and strain into highball glass. Fill with carbonated water.

GOLDEN FRAPPE

1 cup Orange Juice
2 tablespoons Lemon Juice
1 teaspoon Sugar
1 cup Port
Stir sugar, orange juice, and lemon juice in collins glass. Add crushed ice and Port.

GOLDEN SLIPPER COCKTAIL

¾ oz. Chartreuse (Yellow)
2 oz. Old Mr. Boston Apricot
    Flavored Brandy
Stir with ice and strain into cocktail glass. Float an unbroken egg yolk on top.

GOLF COCKTAIL

1½ oz. Old Mr. Boston Dry
    Gin
¾ oz. Dry Vermouth
2 dashes Bitters
Stir with ice and strain into cocktail glass.

OLD Mr. BOSTON

GRAND ROYAL FIZZ
Juice ¼ Orange
Juice ½ Lemon
1 teaspoon Powdered Sugar
2 oz. Old Mr. Boston Dry Gin
½ teaspoon Maraschino
2 teaspoons Sweet Cream
Shake with ice and strain into highball glass over two cubes of ice. Fill with carbonated water and stir.

GRAPEFRUIT COCKTAIL
1 oz. Grapefruit Juice
1 oz. Old Mr. Boston Dry Gin
1 teaspoon Maraschino
Shake with ice and strain into cocktail glass. Serve with a cherry.

GRAPEFRUIT NOG
1½ oz. Old Mr. Boston
    Five Star Brandy
½ cup Unsweetened
    Grapefruit Juice
1 oz. Lemon Juice
1 tablespoon Honey
1 Whole Egg
Blend all ingredients with a cup of crushed ice at low speed and pour into collins glass over ice cubes.

GRAPE VODKA FROTH
1½ oz. Old Mr. Boston
    Vodka
1 oz. Grape Juice
1 Egg White
1 oz. Lemon Juice
Shake with ice and strain into old-fashioned glass over ice cubes.

GRASSHOPPER COCKTAIL
¾ oz. Old Mr. Boston
    Crème de Menthe (Green)
¾ oz. Old Mr. Boston
    Crème de Cacao (White)
¾ oz. Light Sweet Cream
Shake with ice and strain into cocktail glass.

GREENBACK
1½ oz. Old Mr. Boston
    Dry Gin
1 oz. Old Mr. Boston
    Crème de Menthe (Green)
1 oz. Lemon Juice
Shake with ice and strain into old-fashioned glass over ice cubes.

GREEN DEVIL
1½ oz. Old Mr. Boston
    Dry Gin
1½ teaspoon Old Mr. Boston
    Crème de Menthe (Green)
1 tablespoon Lime Juice
Shake with ice and strain into old-fashioned glass over ice cubes. Decorate with mint leaves.

GREEN DRAGON COCKTAIL
Juice ½ Lemon
½ oz. Kümmel
½ oz. Mr. Boston Crème de
    Menthe (Green)
1½ oz. Old Mr. Boston
    Dry Gin
4 dashes Orange Bitters
Shake with ice and strain into cocktail glass.

OLD Mr. BOSTON

GREEN FIZZ

1 teaspoon Powdered Sugar
1 Egg White
Juice ½ Lemon
2 oz. Old Mr. Boston Dry Gin
1 teaspoon Old Mr. Boston
    Crème de Menthe (Green)
*Shake with ice and strain into
highball glass over two cubes
of ice. Fill with carbonated
water and stir.*

GREEN HORNET (DRY)

*Into a collins glass pour 2 oz.
Old Mr. Boston Lime Vodka
over ice cubes. Fill with Wink
soda, stir, and add a half-
slice of lime.*

GREEN OPAL COCKTAIL

½ oz. Old Mr. Boston
    Dry Gin
½ oz. Old Mr. Boston
    Anisette
1 oz. Absinthe Substitute
*Shake with ice and strain into
cocktail glass.*

GREEN SWIZZLE

*Make same as Gin Swizzle on
page 64 and add 1 tablespoon
Old Mr. Boston Crème de
Menthe (Green). If desired,
rum, brandy, or whiskey may
be substituted for the gin.*

GRENADINE RICKEY

Juice ½ Lime
1½ oz. Grenadine
*Pour into highball glass over
ice cubes and fill with carbonated water. Stir. Put piece
of lime in glass.*

GYPSY COCKTAIL

1½ oz. Sweet Vermouth
1½ oz. Old Mr. Boston
    Dry Gin
*Stir with ice and strain into
cocktail glass. Serve with a
cherry.*

HAIR RAISER COCKTAIL
1½ oz. Old Mr. Boston
    100 Proof Vodka
½ oz. Old Mr. Boston
    Rock and Rye
1 tablespoon Lemon Juice
Shake with ice and strain into cocktail glass.

HARLEM COCKTAIL
¾ oz. Pineapple Juice
1½ oz. Old Mr. Boston
    Dry Gin
½ teaspoon Maraschino
Shake with ice and strain into cocktail glass. Decorate with two pineapple chunks.

HARVARD COCKTAIL
1½ oz. Old Mr. Boston
    Five Star Brandy
¾ oz. Sweet Vermouth
1 dash Bitters
1 teaspoon Grenadine
2 teaspoons Lemon Juice
Shake with ice and strain into cocktail glass.

HARVARD COOLER
Into collins glass put ½ teaspoon powdered sugar and 2 oz. carbonated water. **Stir.** *Then add ice cubes and 2 oz. Apple Brandy. Fill with carbonated water or ginger ale and stir again. Insert spiral of orange or lemon peel (or both) and dangle end over rim of glass.*

HARVEY WALLBANGER
1 oz. Old Mr. Boston Vodka
4 oz. Orange Juice
Pour into collins glass over ice cubes. Stir. Float ½ oz. Galliano on top.

HASTY COCKTAIL
¾ oz. Dry Vermouth
1½ oz. Old Mr. Boston
    Dry Gin
¼ teaspoon Absinthe
    Substitute
1 teaspoon Grenadine
Stir with ice and strain into cocktail glass.

HAVANA COCKTAIL
1½ oz. Pineapple Juice
½ teaspoon Lemon Juice
¾ oz. Old Mr. Boston Rum
Shake with ice and strain into cocktail glass.

HAWAIIAN COCKTAIL
2 oz. Old Mr. Boston Dry Gin
1 tablespoon Pineapple Juice
½ oz. Old Mr. Boston
  Triple Sec
Shake with ice and strain into cocktail glass.

HEADLESS HORSEMAN
2 oz. Old Mr. Boston Vodka
3 dashes Bitters
Pour into collins glass and add several cubes of ice. Fill with dry ginger ale, and stir. Decorate with slice of orange.

HIGHBALLS
See Index on page 205 for complete list of Highball recipes.

HIGHLAND COOLER
Into collins glass, put ½ teaspoon powdered sugar and 2 oz. carbonated water. Stir. Then add ice cubes and 2 oz. Desmond & Duff Scotch Whisky. Fill with carbonated water or ginger ale and stir again. Insert spiral of orange or lemon peel (or both) and dangle end over rim of glass.

HIGHLAND FLING COCKTAIL
¾ oz. Sweet Vermouth
1½ oz. Desmond & Duff
  Scotch Whisky
2 dashes Orange Bitters
Stir with ice and strain into cocktail glass. Serve with an olive.

HILL BILLY HIGHBALL
2 oz. Georgia Moon Corn
  Whiskey
Pour into highball glass over ice cubes and fill with Mountain Dew. Then add twist of lemon peel, if desired, and stir.

HOFFMAN HOUSE COCKTAIL
¾ oz. Dry Vermouth
1½ oz. Old Mr. Boston
  Dry Gin
2 dashes Orange Bitters
Stir with ice and strain into cocktail glass. Serve with an olive.

HOKKAIDO COCKTAIL
1½ oz. Old Mr. Boston
  Dry Gin
1 oz. Sake
½ oz. Old Mr. Boston
  Triple Sec
Shake with ice and strain into cocktail glass.

HOLE-IN-ONE COCKTAIL
1¾ oz. Desmond & Duff
  Scotch Whisky
¾ oz. Dry Vermouth
¼ teaspoon Lemon Juice
1 dash Orange Bitters
Shake with ice and strain into cocktail glass.

HOMESTEAD COCKTAIL
1½ oz. Old Mr. Boston
  Dry Gin
¾ oz. Sweet Vermouth
Stir with ice and strain into cocktail glass and serve with slice of orange.

OLD Mr. BOSTON

HONEYMOON COCKTAIL
¾ oz. Benedictine
¾ oz. Apple Brandy
Juice ½ Lemon
1 teaspoon Old Mr. Boston
    Triple Sec
Shake with ice and strain into cocktail glass.

HONOLULU COCKTAIL No. 1
1 dash Bitters
¼ teaspoon Orange Juice
¼ teaspoon Pineapple Juice
¼ teaspoon Lemon Juice
½ teaspoon Powdered Sugar
1½ oz. Old Mr. Boston
    Dry Gin
Shake with ice and strain into cocktail glass.

HONOLULU COCKTAIL No. 2
¾ oz. Old Mr. Boston
    Dry Gin
¾ oz. Maraschino
¾ oz. Benedictine
Stir with ice and strain into cocktail glass.

HOOT MON COCKTAIL
¾ oz. Sweet Vermouth
1½ oz. Desmond & Duff
    Scotch Whisky
1 teaspoon Benedictine
Stir with ice and strain into cocktail glass. Twist lemon peel and drop in glass.

HOP TOAD COCKTAIL
Juice ½ Lime
¾ oz. Old Mr. Boston
    Apricot Flavored Brandy
¾ oz. Old Mr. Boston Rum
Stir with ice and strain into cocktail glass.

HORSE'S NECK
(WITH A KICK)
Peel rind of whole lemon in spiral fashion and put in collins glass with one end hanging over the rim. Fill glass with ice cubes. Add 2 oz. Old Thompson Blended Whiskey. Then fill with ginger ale and stir well.

HOT BRANDY FLIP
1 Whole Egg
1 teaspoon Powdered Sugar
1½ oz. Old Mr. Boston
    Five Star Brandy
Beat egg, sugar, and brandy and pour into mug and fill with hot milk. Stir. Sprinkle nutmeg on top.

HOT BRICK TODDY
Into hot whiskey glass, put:
1 teaspoon Butter
1 teaspoon Powdered Sugar
3 pinches Cinnamon
1 oz. Hot Water
Dissolve thoroughly. Then add:
1½ oz. Old Thompson
    Blended Whiskey
Fill with boiling water and stir.

HOT BUTTERED RUM

Put lump of sugar into hot whiskey glass and fill two-thirds with boiling water. Add square of butter and 2 oz. Old Mr. Boston Rum. *Stir and sprinkle nutmeg on top.*

HOT BUTTERED WINE

For each serving heat ½ cup muscatel. Add ¼ cup water just to simmering; do not boil. Preheat mug or cup with boiling water. Pour heated wine mixture into mug and add 1 teaspoon butter and 2 teaspoons maple syrup. Stir and sprinkle nutmeg on top. Serve at once.

HOT DRINKS

See Index on page 205 for complete list of Hot Drink recipes.

HOT ITALIAN

6 oz. very warm Orange
    Juice
3 oz. Amaretto di Saronno
Pour orange juice into a stemmed wine glass or mug, add Amaretto di Saronno *and garnish with cinnamon stick as stirrer.*

HOT PANTS

1½ oz. Gavilan Tequila
½ oz. Old Mr. Boston
    Peppermint Schnapps
1 tablespoon Unsweetened
    Grapefruit Juice
1 teaspoon Powdered Sugar
Shake with ice cubes and pour into old-fashioned glass rimmed with salt.

HOT SPRINGS COCKTAIL

1½ oz. Dry White Wine
1 tablespoon Pineapple Juice
½ teaspoon Maraschino
1 dash Orange Bitters
Shake with ice and strain into cocktail glass.

HOTEL PLAZA COCKTAIL

¾ oz. Sweet Vermouth
¾ oz. Dry Vermouth
¾ oz. Old Mr. Boston
    Dry Gin
Stir with ice and strain into cocktail glass. Decorate with a crushed slice of pineapple.

H.P.W. COCKTAIL

1½ teaspoons Dry Vermouth
1½ teaspoons Sweet
    Vermouth
1½ oz. Old Mr. Boston
    Dry Gin
Stir with ice and strain into cocktail glass. Add a twist of orange peel.

HUDSON BAY

1 oz. Old Mr. Boston Dry Gin
½ oz. Old Mr. Boston
    Wild Cherry Flavored
    Brandy
1½ teaspoons
    151 Proof Rum
1 tablespoon Orange Juice
1½ teaspoons Lime Juice
Shake with ice and strain into cocktail glass.

OLD Mr. BOSTON

HULA-HULA COCKTAIL
¾ oz. Orange Juice
1½ oz. Old Mr. Boston
   Dry Gin
¼ teaspoon Powdered Sugar
*Shake with ice and strain into
cocktail glass.*

HUNTSMAN COCKTAIL
1½ oz. Old Mr. Boston
   Vodka
½ oz. Jamaica Rum
Juice ½ Lime
Powdered Sugar to taste
*Shake with ice and strain into
cocktail glass.*

HURRICANE
1 oz. Old Mr. Boston Dark
   Rum
1 oz. Old Mr. Boston
   Light Rum
1 tablespoon Passion Fruit
   Syrup
2 teaspoons Lime Juice
*Shake with ice and strain into
cocktail glass.*

HYATT'S JAMAICAN
BANANA*
½ oz. Mr. Boston White
   Rum
½ oz. Mr. Boston Crème
   de Cacao (White)
½ oz. Mr. Boston Crème
   de Banana
2 scoops vanilla ice cream
1 oz. half and half
whole banana
*Blend and garnish with 2
slices banana, strawberry and
nutmeg.*

*Hyatt Regency Hotel, Dallas, Texas

ICE CREAM FLIP

1 Whole Egg
1 oz. Maraschino
1 oz. Mr. Boston Triple Sec
1 small scoop Vanilla
    Ice Cream

Shake with ice and strain into flip glass. Sprinkle a little nutmeg on top.

IDEAL COCKTAIL

1 oz. Dry Vermouth
1 oz. Old Mr. Boston Dry Gin
¼ teaspoon Maraschino
½ teaspoon Grapefruit or
    Lemon Juice

Shake with ice and strain into cocktail glass. Serve with a cherry.

IMPERIAL COCKTAIL

1½ oz. Dry Vermouth
1½ oz. Old Mr. Boston
    Dry Gin
½ teaspoon Maraschino
1 dash Bitters

Stir with ice and strain into cocktail glass. Serve with a cherry.

IMPERIAL FIZZ

Juice ½ Lemon
½ oz. Old Mr. Boston Rum
1½ oz. Old Thompson
    Blended Whiskey
1 teaspoon Powdered Sugar

Shake with ice and strain into highball glass. Add two ice cubes. Fill with carbonated water and stir.

INCIDER COCKTAIL

1½ oz. Old Thompson
    Blended Whiskey
Apple Cider

Mix 1½ oz. of Old Thompson Blended Whiskey with a generous helping of Apple Cider. Serve over ice in old-fashioned glass and garnish with a slice of apple.

INCOME TAX COCKTAIL

1½ teaspoons Dry Vermouth
1½ teaspoons Sweet
    Vermouth
1 oz. Old Mr. Boston Dry Gin
1 dash Bitters
Juice ¼ Orange

Shake with ice and strain into cocktail glass.

IRISH COFFEE

Into a stemmed glass or cup rimmed with sugar, pour 1½ oz. Irish Whisky. Fill to within ½ inch of top with strong, hot black coffee. Cover surface to brim with chilled whipped cream.

IRISH RICKEY

Juice ½ Lime
1½ oz. Irish Whisky

Fill highball glass with carbonated water and ice cubes. Stir. Add piece of lime.

OLD Mr. BOSTON

IRISH SHILLELAGH

Juice ½ Lemon
1 teaspoon Powdered Sugar
1½ oz. Irish Whisky
1 tablespoon Old Mr. Boston
    Sloe Gin
1 tablespoon Old Mr. Boston
    Rum

Shake with ice and strain into punch glass. Decorate with fresh raspberries, strawberries, a cherry, and two peach slices.

IRISH WHISKY COCKTAIL

½ teaspoon Old Mr. Boston
    Triple Sec
½ teaspoon Absinthe
    Substitute
¼ teaspoon Maraschino
1 dash Bitters
2 oz. Irish Whisky

Stir with ice and strain into cocktail glass. Serve with an olive.

IRISH WHISKY HIGHBALL

Pour into highball glass 2 oz. Irish Whisky over ice cubes and fill with ginger ale or carbonated water. Add twist of lemon peel, if desired, and stir.

ITALIAN COFFEE (AMARETTO CAFE)

Pour 1 oz. Amaretto di Saronno into hot coffee. Stir and enjoy. For an extra treat, top the coffee with whipped cream.

ITALIAN SOMBRERO

1½ oz. Amaretto Di Saronno
3 oz. Sweet Cream
Put in a blender or shake well. Serve over ice cubes or straight up in stem champagne glass.

J

JACK-IN-THE-BOX COCKTAIL
1 oz. Apple Brandy
1 oz. Pineapple Juice
1 dash Bitters
Shake with ice and strain into cocktail glass.

JACK ROSE COCKTAIL
1½ oz. Apple Brandy
Juice ½ Lime
1 teaspoon Grenadine
Shake with ice and strain into cocktail glass.

JADE
1½ oz. Old Mr. Boston
    Rum (Dark)
½ teaspoon Old Mr. Boston
    Crème de Menthe (Green)
½ teaspoon Old Mr. Boston
    Triple Sec
1 tablespoon Lime Juice
1 teaspoon Powdered Sugar
Shake with ice and strain into cocktail glass. Add lime slice.

JAMAICA COFFEE
1 oz. Old Mr. Boston Coffee
    Flavored Brandy
¾ oz. Old Mr. Boston Rum
Hot Coffee
Serve in mug slightly sweetened. Top with whipped cream and sprinkle with nutmeg.

JAMAICA GLOW COCKTAIL
1 oz. Old Mr. Boston Dry Gin
1 tablespoon Claret
1 tablespoon Orange Juice
1 teaspoon Jamaica Rum
Shake with ice and strain into cocktail glass.

JAMAICA GRANITO
1 small scoop Lemon or
    Orange Sherbet
1½ oz. Old Mr. Boston
    Five Star Brandy
1 oz. Old Mr. Boston
    Triple Sec
Combine in collins glass and fill balance with carbonated water and stir. Sprinkle nutmeg on top.

JAMAICA HOP
1 oz. Old Mr. Boston Coffee
    Flavored Brandy
1 oz. Old Mr. Boston Crème
    de Cacao (White)
1 oz. Light Cream
Shake well with ice and strain into cocktail glass.

JAPANESE

2 oz. Old Mr. Boston
    Five Star Brandy
1½ teaspoons Orgeat Syrup
1 tablespoon Lime Juice
1 dash Bitters
Shake with ice and strain into cocktail glass. Add twist of lime peel.

JAPANESE FIZZ

Juice ½ Lemon
1 teaspoon Powdered Sugar
1½ oz. Old Thompson
    Blended Whiskey
1 tablespoon Port
1 Egg White
Shake with ice and strain into highball glass over two cubes of ice. Fill with carbonated water and stir. Serve with slice of pineapple.

JEAN LAFITTE COCKTAIL

1 oz. Old Mr. Boston Dry Gin
½ oz. Old Mr. Boston
    Triple Sec
½ oz. Absinthe Substitute
1 teaspoon Powdered Sugar
1 Egg Yolk
Shake with ice and strain into cocktail glass.

JERSEY LIGHTNING COCKTAIL

1½ oz. Apple Brandy
½ oz. Sweet Vermouth
Juice 1 lime
Shake with ice and strain into cocktail glass.

JEWEL COCKTAIL

¾ oz. Chartreuse (Green)
¾ oz. Sweet Vermouth
¾ oz. Old Mr. Boston
    Dry Gin
1 dash Orange Bitters
Stir with ice and strain into cocktail glass. Serve with a cherry.

JEYPLAK COCKTAIL

1½ oz. Old Mr. Boston
    Dry Gin
¾ oz. Sweet Vermouth
¼ teaspoon Absinthe
    Substitute
Stir with ice and strain into cocktail glass. Serve with a cherry.

JOCKEY CLUB COCKTAIL

1 dash Bitters
¼ teaspoon Old Mr. Boston
    Crème de Cacao (White)
Juice ¼ Lemon
1½ oz. Old Mr. Boston
    Dry Gin
Shake with ice and strain into cocktail glass.

JOCOSE JULEP

2½ oz. Old Kentucky Tavern
  Bourbon Whiskey
½ oz. Old Mr. Boston Crème
  de Menthe (Green)
1 oz. Lime Juice
1 teaspoon Sugar
5 chopped Mint Leaves
*Combine all ingredients in a
blender without ice. Pour into
collins glass over ice cubes.
Fill with carbonated water
and decorate with sprig of
mint.*

JOHN COLLINS

Juice ½ Lemon
1 teaspoon Powdered Sugar
2 oz. Old Thompson
  Blended Whiskey
*Shake with ice and strain into
collins glass. Add several cubes
of ice, fill with carbonated
water, and stir. Decorate with
slice of orange, lemon, and a
cherry. Serve with straws.*

JOHNNIE COCKTAIL

¾ oz. Old Mr. Boston
  Triple Sec
1½ oz. Old Mr. Boston .
  Sloe Gin
1 teaspoon Old Mr. Boston
  Anisette
*Shake with ice and strain into
cocktail glass.*

JOULOUVILLE

1 oz. Old Mr. Boston Dry Gin
½ oz. Apple Brandy
1½ teaspoons Sweet
  Vermouth
1 tablespoon Lemon Juice
2 dashes Grenadine
*Shake with ice and strain into
cocktail glass.*

JOURNALIST COCKTAIL

1½ teaspoons Dry Vermouth
1½ teaspoons Sweet
  Vermouth
1½ oz. Old Mr. Boston
  Dry Gin
½ teaspoon Lemon Juice
½ teaspoon Old Mr. Boston
  Triple Sec
1 dash Bitters
*Shake with ice and strain into
cocktail glass.*

JUDGE JR. COCKTAIL

¾ oz. Old Mr. Boston
  Dry Gin
¾ oz. Old Mr. Boston Rum
Juice ¼ Lemon
½ teaspoon Powdered Sugar
¼ teaspoon Grenadine
*Shake with ice and strain into
cocktail glass.*

JUDGETTE COCKTAIL

¾ oz. Old Mr. Boston
  Peach Flavored Brandy
¾ oz. Old Mr. Boston
  Dry Gin
¾ oz. Dry Vermouth
Juice ¼ Lime
*Shake with ice and strain into
cocktail glass. Serve with a
cherry.*

JULEPS

*See Index on page 206 for
complete list of Julep recipes.*

K

KANGAROO COCKTAIL

1½ oz. Old Mr. Boston
    Vodka
¾ oz. Dry Vermouth
Shake with ice and strain into cocktail glass. Serve with twist of lemon peel.

K.C.B. COCKTAIL

½ oz. Kümmel
1½ oz. Old Mr. Boston
    Dry Gin
¼ teaspoon Mr. Boston
    Apricot Flavored Brandy
¼ teaspoon Lemon Juice
Shake with ice and strain into cocktail glass. Add twist of lemon peel.

KENTUCKY COCKTAIL

¾ oz. Pineapple Juice
1½ oz. Old Kentucky Tavern
    Bourbon Whiskey
Shake with ice and strain into cocktail glass.

KENTUCKY COLONEL COCKTAIL

½ oz. Benedictine
1½ oz. Old Kentucky Tavern
    Bourbon Whiskey
Stir with ice and strain into cocktail glass. Add twist of lemon peel.

KING COLE COCKTAIL

1 slice Orange
1 slice Pineapple
½ teaspoon Powdered Sugar
Muddle well in old-fashioned glass and add:
2 oz. Old Thompson
    Blended Whiskey
2 Ice Cubes
Stir well.

KIR COCKTAIL

3 oz. Dry White Wine
¾ oz. Mr. Boston Creme
    de Cassis
Pour Wine over ice in an old-fashioned glass. Add Creme de Cassis, a twist of lemon and stir.

KISS-IN-THE DARK COCKTAIL

¾ oz. Old Mr. Boston
    Dry Gin
¾ oz. Old Mr. Boston Wild
    Cherry Flavored Brandy
¾ oz. Dry Vermouth
Stir with ice and strain into cocktail glass.

KISS THE BOYS GOODBYE

¾ oz. Old Mr. Boston
    Sloe Gin
¾ oz. Old Mr. Boston
    Five Star Brandy
½ Egg White
Juice 1 Lemon
Shake with ice and strain into cocktail glass.

KLONDIKE COOLER

Into collins glass, put ½ teaspoon powdered sugar and 2 oz. carbonated water. Stir and fill glass with ice and add
2 oz. Old Thompson Blended Whiskey.
Fill with carbonated water or ginger ale and stir again. Insert spiral of orange or lemon peel (or both) and dangle end over rim of glass.

KNICKERBOCKER COCKTAIL

¼ teaspoon Sweet Vermouth
¾ oz. Dry Vermouth
1½ oz. Old Mr. Boston Dry Gin
Stir with ice, strain into cocktail glass. Add twist of lemon peel.

KNICKERBOCKER SPECIAL COCKTAIL

1 teaspoon Raspberry Syrup
1 teaspoon Lemon Juice
1 tesapoon Orange Juice
2 oz. Old Mr. Boston Rum
½ teaspoon Old Mr. Boston Triple Sec
Shake with ice and strain into cocktail glass. Decorate with small slice of pineapple.

KNOCK-OUT COCKTAIL

½ oz. Absinthe Substitute
¾ oz. Old Mr. Boston Dry Gin
¾ oz. Dry Vermouth
1 teaspoon Old Mr. Boston Crème de Menthe (White)
Stir with ice and strain into cocktail glass. Serve with a cherry.

KRETCHMA COCKTAIL

1 oz. Old Mr. Boston Vodka
1 oz. Old Mr. Boston Crème de Cacao (White)
1 tablespoon Lemon Juice
1 dash Grenadine
Shake with ice and strain into cocktail glass.

KUP'S INDISPENSABLE COCKTAIL

½ oz. Sweet Vermouth
½ oz. Dry Vermouth
1½ oz. Old Mr. Boston Dry Gin
1 dash Bitters
Stir with ice and strain into cocktail glass.

LADIES' COCKTAIL

1¾ oz. Old Thompson
    Blended Whiskey
½ teaspoon Old Mr. Boston
    Anisette
2 dashes Bitters
Stir with ice and strain into cocktail glass. Serve with a pineapple stick on top.

LADY BE GOOD

1½ oz. Old Mr. Boston
    Five Star Brandy
½ oz. Old Mr. Boston
    Crème de Menthe (White)
½ oz. Sweet Vermouth
Shake with ice and strain into cocktail glass.

LADY FINGER

1 oz. Old Mr. Boston Dry Gin
½ oz. Kirschwasser
1 oz. Old Mr. Boston Wild
    Cherry Flavored Brandy
Shake with ice and strain into cocktail glass.

LADY LOVE FIZZ

1 teaspoon Powdered Sugar
Juice ½ Lemon
1 Egg White
2 oz. Old Mr. Boston Dry Gin
2 teaspoons Sweet Cream
Shake with ice and strain into highball glass over two cubes of ice. Fill with carbonated water and stir.

LA JOLLA

1½ oz. Old Mr. Boston
    Five Star Brandy
½ oz. Old Mr. Boston
    Crème de Banana
1 teaspoon Orange Juice
2 teaspoons Lemon Juice
Shake with ice and strain into cocktail glass.

LASKY COCKTAIL

¾ oz. Grape Juice
¾ oz. Swedish Punch
¾ oz. Old Mr. Boston
    Dry Gin
Shake with ice and strain into cocktail glass.

LAWHILL COCKTAIL
¾ oz. Dry Vermouth
1½ oz. Old Thompson
    Blended Whiskey
¼ teaspoon Absinthe
    Substitute
¼ teaspoon Maraschino
1 dash Bitters
Stir with ice and strain into cocktail glass.

LEAP FROG HIGHBALL
Juice ½ Lemon
2 oz. Old Mr. Boston Dry Gin
Pour into highball glass over ice cubes and fill with ginger ale. Stir.

LEAVE-IT-TO-ME COCKTAIL NO. 1
½ oz. Old Mr. Boston
    Apricot Flavored Brandy
½ oz. Dry Vermouth
1 oz. Old Mr. Boston Dry Gin
¼ teaspoon Lemon Juice
¼ teaspoon Grenadine
Shake with ice and strain into cocktail glass.

LEAVE-IT-TO-ME COCKTAIL NO. 2
1 teaspoon Raspberry Syrup
1 teaspoon Lemon Juice
¼ teaspoon Maraschino
1½ oz. Old Mr. Boston
    Dry Gin
Stir with ice and strain into cocktail glass.

LEMON SQUASH
1 Lemon, peeled and
    quartered
2 teaspoons Powdered Sugar
Muddle well in collins glass until juice is well extracted. Then fill glass with ice. Add carbonated water and stir. Decorate with fruits.

LEAP YEAR COCKTAIL
1¼ oz. Old Mr. Boston
    Dry Gin
½ oz. Orange Flavored Gin
½ oz. Sweet Vermouth
¼ teaspoon Lemon Juice
Shake with ice and strain into cocktail glass.

LEMONADE (CARBONATED)

2 teaspoons Powdered Sugar
Juice 1 Lemon

Dissolve in collins glass, then add ice and enough carbonated water to fill glass and stir. Decorate with slices of orange and lemon, and a cherry. Serve with straws.

LEMONADE (CLARET)

2 teaspoons Powdered Sugar
Juice 1 Lemon

Dissolve in collins glass, then add ice and enough water to fill glass, leaving room to float 2 oz. Claret. Decorate with slices of orange and lemon, and a cherry. Serve with straws.

LEMONADE (EGG)

Juice 1 Lemon
2 teaspoons Powdered Sugar
1 Whole Egg

Shake and strain into collins glass over ice cubes. Add enough water to fill glass. Serve with straws.

LEMONADE (FRUIT)

Juice 1 Lemon
2 teaspoons Powdered Sugar
1 oz. Raspberry Syrup

Combine in collins glass. Add ice cubes and enough water to fill glass and stir. Decorate with slices of orange and lemon, and a cherry. Serve with straws.

LEMONADE (GOLDEN)

Juice 1 Lemon
2 teaspoons Powdered Sugar
1 Egg Yolk
6 oz. Water

Shake with ice and strain into collins glass. Decorate with slices of orange and lemon, and a cherry.

LEMONADE (MODERN)

1 Lemon
2 teaspoons Powdered Sugar
1½ oz. Sherry
1 oz. Old Mr. Boston
    Sloe Gin

Cut lemon in quarters and muddle well with sugar. Add sherry and sloe gin. Shake with ice and strain into collins glass. Fill glass with carbonated water.

LEMONADE (PLAIN)

2 teaspoons Powdered Sugar
Juice 1 Lemon

Stir. Then fill collins glass with ice. Add enough water to fill glass and stir well. Decorate with slices of orange and lemon and a cherry.

LIBERTY COCKTAIL

¾ oz. Old Mr. Boston Rum
1½ oz. Apple Brandy
¼ teaspoon Sugar Syrup
Stir with ice and strain into cocktail glass.

LIL NAUE

1 oz. Old Mr. Boston
  Five Star Brandy
½ oz. Port
½ oz. Old Mr. Boston
  Apricot Flavored Brandy
1 teaspoon Powdered Sugar
1 Egg Yolk
Shake with ice and strain into wine glass. Sprinkle cinnamon on top.

LIMEADE

Juice 3 Limes
3 teaspoons Powdered Sugar
Combine in collins glass, then add ice and enough water to fill glass. Stir and drop a wedge of lime in glass. Add a cherry. Serve with straws.

LIME GIANT

Put ice cubes in collins glass and add 2 oz. Old Mr. Boston Lime Vodka. *Fill with lemon and lime soda. Decorate with slice of lime.*

LIMESTONE

1½ oz. Yellowstone Bourbon
Collins Mix
Lime Juice
In ice filled highball glass, pour 1½ oz. Yellowstone Bourbon, fill glass with Collins mix and add lime Juice to taste. Enjoy it stone cold.

LIMEY

1 oz. Old Mr. Boston Rum
1 oz. Lime Liqueur
½ oz. Old Mr. Boston
  Triple Sec
2 teaspoons Lime Juice
Combine ingredients half a cup of crushed ice in a blender. Blend at low speed and pour into champagne glass. Add a twist of lime peel.

LINSTEAD COCKTAIL

1 oz. Old Thompson
  Blended Whiskey
1 oz. Pineapple Juice
½ teaspoon Powdered Sugar
¼ teaspoon Absinthe
  Substitute
¼ teaspoon Lemon Juice
Shake with ice and strain into cocktail glass.

LITTLE DEVIL COCKTAIL

Juice ¼ Lemon
1½ teaspoons Old Mr. Boston
  Triple Sec
¾ oz. Old Mr. Boston Rum
¾ oz. Old Mr. Boston
  Dry Gin
Shake with ice and strain into cocktail glass.

LITTLE PRINCESS COCKTAIL

1½ oz. Sweet Vermouth
1½ oz. Old Mr. Boston Rum
Stir with ice and strain into cocktail glass.

OLD Mr. BOSTON

LONDON BUCK

2 oz. Old Mr. Boston Dry Gin
Juice ½ Lemon
Pour over ice cubes in high-ball glass. Fill with ginger ale and stir.

LONDON COCKTAIL

2 oz. Old Mr. Boston Dry Gin
2 dashes Orange Bitters
½ teaspoon Sugar Syrup
½ teaspoon Maraschino
Stir with ice and strain into cocktail glass. Add twist of lemon peel.

LONDON SPECIAL COCKTAIL

Put a large twist of orange peel into champagne glass. Add 1 lump sugar and 2 dashes bitters. Fill with well-chilled champagne and stir.

LONE TREE COCKTAIL

¾ oz. Sweet Vermouth
1½ oz. Old Mr. Boston
     Dry Gin
Stir with ice and strain into cocktail glass.

LONE TREE COOLER

Into collins glass, put:
½ teaspoon Powdered Sugar
2 oz. Carbonated Water
Stir and fill glass with ice and add:
2 oz. Old Mr. Boston Dry Gin
1 tablespoon Dry Vermouth
Fill with carbonated water or ginger ale and stir again. Insert spiral of orange or lemon peel (or both) and dangle end over rim of glass.

LOOK OUT BELOW

1½ oz. 151 Proof Rum
Juice ¼ Lime
1 teaspoon Grenadine
Shake with ice and strain into old-fashioned glass over ice cubes.

LOS ANGELES COCKTAIL

Juice ½ Lemon
1 teaspoon Powdered Sugar
1 Whole Egg
¼ teaspoon Sweet Vermouth
1½ oz. Old Thompson
     Blended Whiskey
Shake with ice and strain into flip glass.

LOVE COCKTAIL

2 oz. Old Mr. Boston Sloe Gin
1 Egg White
½ teaspoon Lemon Juice
½ teaspoon Raspberry Juice
Shake with ice and strain into cocktail glass.

LOVING CUP

4 teaspoons Powdered Sugar
6 oz. Carbonated Water
1 oz. Old Mr. Boston
   Triple Sec
2 oz. Old Mr. Boston
   Five Star Brandy
1 pt. Claret
Fill large glass pitcher with ice and stir in the ingredients. Decorate with as many fruits as available and also rind of cucumber inserted on each side of pitcher. Top with small bunch of mint sprigs.

LUGGER

1 oz. Old Mr. Boston
   Five Star Brandy
1 oz. Apple Brandy
1 dash Old Mr. Boston
   Apricot Flavored Brandy
Shake with ice and strain into cocktail glass.

LUXURY COCKTAIL

3 oz. Old Mr. Boston
   Five Star Brandy
2 dashes Orange Bitters
3 oz. Well-Chilled
   Champagne
Stir and pour into saucer champagne glass.

M

Maiden's Blush Cocktail

¼ teaspoon Lemon Juice
1 teaspoon Old Mr. Boston
　Triple Sec
1 teaspoon Grenadine
1½ oz. Old Mr. Boston
　Dry Gin
Shake with ice and strain into cocktail glass.

Maiden's Prayer

1½ oz. Old Mr. Boston
　Dry Gin
½ oz. Old Mr. Boston
　Triple Sec
1 oz. Lemon Juice
Shake with ice and strain into cocktail glass.

Mai-Tai

½ teaspoon Powdered Sugar
2 oz. Old Mr. Boston Rum
1 oz. Old Mr. Boston
　Triple Sec
1 tablespoon Orgeat or
　Almond Flavored Syrup
1 tablespoon Grenadine
1 tablespoon Lime Juice
Shake with ice and strain into large old-fashioned glass about ⅓ full with crushed ice. Decorate with Maraschino cherry speared to wedge of preferably fresh pineapple. For a hair raiser, top with a dash of 151 proof rum and for a real Hawaiian effect float an orchid on each drink. Serve with straws.

Major Bailey

1½ teaspoons Lime Juice
1½ teaspoons Lemon Juice
½ teaspoon Powdered Sugar
12 Mint Leaves
Muddle well and pour into collins glass filled with ice and add 2 oz. Old Mr. Boston Dry Gin. Stir until glass is frosted. Decorate with sprig of mint and serve with straws.

MALMAISON

Juice ½ Lemon
1 oz. Old Mr. Boston Rum
½ oz. Sweet Sherry
Shake with ice and strain into cocktail glass rimmed with Old Mr. Boston Anisette.

MAMIE GILROY

Juice ½ Lime
2 oz. Desmond & Duff
  Scotch Whisky
1 dash Bitters
Pour into collins glass over ice cubes and fill with carbonated water. Stir.

MAMIE TAYLOR

Juice ½ Lime
2 oz. Desmond & Duff
  Scotch Whisky
Fill collins glass with ginger ale and ice. Stir.

MAMIE'S SISTER

Drop the juice of one lime and rind in collins glass, and add 2 oz. Old Mr. Boston Dry Gin. *Fill glass with ginger ale and ice. Stir.*

MANDEVILLE

1½ oz. Old Mr. Boston
  Light Rum
1 oz. Old Mr. Boston
  Dark Rum
1 teaspoon Absinthe
  Substitute
1 tablespoon Lemon Juice
1 tablespoon Cola Drink
¼ teaspoon Grenadine
Shake with ice and strain into old-fashioned glass over ice cubes.

MANHASSET

1½ oz. Old Thompson
  Blended Whiskey
1½ teaspoons Dry Vermouth
1½ teaspoons Sweet
  Vermouth
1 tablespoon Lemon Juice
Shake with ice and strain into cocktail glass.

MANHATTAN COCKTAIL

¾ oz. Sweet Vermouth
1½ oz. Old Thompson
  Blended Whiskey
Stir with ice and strain into cocktail glass. Serve with a cherry.

MANHATTAN COCKTAIL (DRY)

¾ oz. Dry Vermouth
1½ oz. Old Thompson
  Blended Whiskey
Stir with ice and strain into cocktail glass. Serve with an olive.

MANILA FIZZ

2 oz. Old Mr. Boston Dry Gin
1 Whole Egg
1 teaspoon Powdered Sugar
2 oz. Sarsaparilla
Juice 1 Lime or ½ Lemon
Shake with ice and strain into highball glass over two cubes of ice.

Margarita Cocktail

1½ oz. Gavilan Tequila
½ oz. Old Mr. Boston
   Triple Sec
1 oz. Lemon or Lime Juice
Rub rim of cocktail glass with rind of lemon or lime, dip rim in salt. Shake ingredients with ice and strain into the salt-rimmed glass.

Mariposa Cocktail

1 oz. Old Mr. Boston Rum
½ oz. Old Mr. Boston
   Five Star Brandy
1 tablespoon Lemon Juice
1 tablespoon Orange Juice
1 dash Grenadine
Shake with ice and strain into cocktail glass.

Martinez Cocktail

1 dash Orange Bitters
1 oz. Dry Vermouth
¼ teaspoon Old Mr. Boston
   Triple Sec
1 oz. Old Mr. Boston Dry Gin
Stir with ice and strain into cocktail glass. Serve with a cherry.

Martini Cocktail

See Special Martini Section on pages 173 and 174.

Mary Garden Cocktail

1½ oz. Dubonnet
¾ oz. Dry Vermouth
Stir with ice and strain into cocktail glass.

Mary Pickford Cocktail

1 oz. Old Mr. Boston Rum
1 oz. Pineapple Juice
¼ teaspoon Grenadine
¼ teaspoon Maraschino
Shake with ice and strain into cocktail glass.

Maurice Cocktail

Juice ¼ Orange
½ oz. Sweet Vermouth
½ oz. Dry Vermouth
1 oz. Old Mr. Boston Dry Gin
1 dash Bitters
Shake with ice and strain into cocktail glass.

Maxim

1½ oz. Old Mr. Boston
   Dry Gin
1 oz. Dry Vermouth
1 dash Old Mr. Boston
   Crème de Cacao (White)
Shake with ice and strain into cocktail glass.

May Blossom Fizz

1 teaspoon Grenadine
Juice ½ Lemon
2 oz. Swedish Punch
Shake with ice and strain into highball glass over two cubes of ice. Fill with carbonated water and stir.

McClelland Cocktail

¾ oz. Old Mr. Boston
   Triple Sec
1½ oz. Old Mr. Boston
   Sloe Gin
1 dash Orange Bitters
Shake with ice and strain into cocktail glass.

MELON COCKTAIL

2 oz. Old Mr. Boston Dry Gin
¼ teaspoon Lemon Juice
¼ teaspoon Maraschino
Shake with ice and strain into cocktail glass. Serve with a cherry.

MERRY WIDOW COCKTAIL NO. 1

1¼ oz. Old Mr. Boston Dry Gin
1¼ oz. Dry Vermouth
½ teaspoon Benedictine
½ teaspoon Absinthe Substitute
1 dash Orange Bitters
Stir with ice and strain into cocktail glass. Add twist of lemon peel.

MERRY WIDOW COCKTAIL NO. 2

1¼ oz. Maraschino
1¼ oz. Old Mr. Boston Wild Cherry Flavored Brandy
Stir with ice and strain into cocktail glass. Serve with a cherry.

MERRY WIDOW FIZZ

Juice ½ Orange
Juice ½ Lemon
1 Egg White
1 teaspoon Powdered Sugar
1½ oz. Old Mr. Boston Sloe Gin
Shake with ice and strain into highball glass with two cubes ice. Fill with carbonated water and stir.

METROPOLITAN COCKTAIL

1¼ oz. Old Mr. Boston Five Star Brandy
1¼ oz. Sweet Vermouth
½ teaspoon Sugar Syrup
1 dash Bitters
Stir with ice and strain into cocktail glass.

MEXICANA

1½ oz. Gavilan Tequila
1 oz. Lemon Juice
1 tablespoon Pineapple Juice
1 teaspoon Grenadine
Shake with ice and strain into cocktail glass.

MEXICOLA

2 oz. Gavilan Tequila
Juice ½ Lime
Fill collins glass with cubes of ice. Add tequila and lime juice and fill balance with cola and stir.

MIAMI

1½ oz. Old Mr. Boston Rum
½ oz. Old Mr. Boston Crème de Menthe (White)
1 dash Lemon Juice
Shake with ice and strain into cocktail glass.

OLD Mr. BOSTON

MIAMI BEACH COCKTAIL

¾ oz. Desmond & Duff
    Scotch Whisky
¾ oz. Dry Vermouth
¾ oz. Grapefruit Juice
*Shake with ice and strain into
cocktail glass.*

MIDNIGHT COCKTAIL

1 oz. Old Mr. Boston
    Apricot Flavored Brandy
½ oz. Old Mr. Boston
    Triple Sec
1 tablespoon Lemon Juice
*Shake with ice and strain into
cocktail glass.*

MIKADO COCKTAIL

1 oz. Old Mr. Boston
    Five Star Brandy
1 dash Mr. Boston Triple Sec
1 dash Grenadine
1 dash Mr. Boston
    Crème de Noyaux
1 dash Angostura Bitters
*Stir in old-fashioned glass
over ice cubes.*

MILK PUNCH

1 teaspoon Powdered Sugar
2 oz. Old Thompson
    Blended Whiskey
1 cup Milk
*Shake with ice and strain into
collins glass. Sprinkle nutmeg
on top.*

MILLION DOLLAR COCKTAIL

2 teaspoons Pineapple Juice
1 teaspoon Grenadine
1 Egg White
¾ oz. Sweet Vermouth
1½ oz. Old Mr. Boston
    Dry Gin
*Shake with ice and strain into
cocktail glass.*

MILLIONAIRE COCKTAIL

1 Egg White
¼ teaspoon Grenadine
½ oz. Old Mr. Boston
    Triple Sec
1½ oz. Old Thompson
    Blended Whiskey
*Shake with ice and strain into
cocktail glass.*

MINT COLLINS

Juice ½ Lemon
2 oz. Old Mr. Boston
    Mint Flavored Gin
*Shake with ice and strain into
collins glass. Add several
cubes of ice, fill with carbonated water, and stir. Decorate with slices of lemon and
orange and a cherry. Serve
with straws.*

MINT GIN COCKTAIL

1 oz. Old Mr. Boston
    Mint Flavored Gin
1 oz. White Port
1½ teaspoons Dry Vermouth
Stir with ice and strain into cocktail glass.

MINT HIGHBALL

2 oz. Old Mr. Boston
    Crème de Menthe (Green)
Pour into highball glass over ice cubes and fill with ginger ale or carbonated water. Add twist of lemon peel, if desired, and stir.

MINT JULEP

Into a silver mug or collins glass muddle 4 sprigs of mint, 1 teaspoon powdered sugar, and 2 teaspoons water. Fill glass or mug with ice and 2½ oz. Old Kentucky Tavern Bourbon Whiskey *and stir until glass is frosted. Decorate with slices of orange, lemon, pineapple, and a cherry. Insert five or six sprigs of mint on top. Serve with straws.*

MINT JULEP (SOUTHERN STYLE)

Into a silver mug or collins glass, dissolve one teaspoon powdered sugar with two teaspoons of water. Then fill with finely shaved ice and add 2½ oz. Old Kentucky Tavern Bourbon Whiskey. *Stir until glass is heavily frosted adding more ice if necessary. (Do not hold glass with hand while stirring.) Decorate with five or six sprigs of fresh mint so that the tops are about two inches above rim of mug or glass. Use short straws so that it will be necessary to bury nose in mint. The mint is intended for odor rather than taste.*

MINT ON ROCKS

Pour 2 oz. Old Mr. Boston Crème de Menthe (Green) *on ice cubes in old-fashioned glass.*

MISSISSIPPI PLANTERS PUNCH

1 tablespoon Powdered Sugar
Juice 1 Lemon
½ oz. Old Mr. Boston
    Rum
½ oz. Old Kentucky Tavern
    Straight Bourbon
    Whiskey
1 oz. Old Mr. Boston Five
    Star Brandy
Shake all ingredients with ice and strain into collins glass with cubed ice. Fill with carbonated water and stir.

MR. MANHATTAN COCKTAIL
Muddle lump of sugar with:
4 sprigs Mint
¼ teaspoon Lemon Juice
1 teaspoon Orange Juice
1½ oz. Old Mr. Boston
    Dry Gin
Shake with ice and strain into cocktail glass.

MOCHA GREENSLEEVES
1½ oz. Greensleeves Mint
    Cream Liqueur
3 oz. Expresso® Coffee
    Liqueur
Shake with ice and serve over rocks.

MOCHA MINT
¾ oz. Old Mr. Boston
    Coffee Flavored Brandy
¾ oz. Old Mr. Boston
    Crème de Cacao (White)
¾ oz. Old Mr. Boston
    Crème de Menthe (White)
Shake with ice and strain into cocktail glass.

MODERN COCKTAIL
1½ oz. Desmond & Duff
    Scotch Whisky
½ teaspoon Lemon Juice
¼ teaspoon Absinthe
    Substitute
½ teaspoon Jamaica Rum
1 dash Orange Bitters
Shake with ice and strain into cocktail glass. Serve with a cherry.

MONTANA
1½ oz. Old Mr. Boston
    Five Star Brandy
1 oz. Port
½ oz. Dry Vermouth
Stir in old-fashioned glass on the rocks.

MONTE CARLO IMPERIAL HIGHBALL
2 oz. Old Mr. Boston Dry Gin
½ oz. Old Mr. Boston
    Crème de Menthe (White)
Juice ¼ Lemon
Shake with ice and strain into highball glass over ice cubes. Fill glass with champagne and stir.

MONTMARTRE COCKTAIL
1¼ oz. Old Mr. Boston
    Dry Gin
½ oz. Sweet Vermouth
½ oz. Old Mr. Boston
    Triple Sec
Stir with ice and strain into cocktail glass. Serve with a cherry.

MONTREAL CLUB BOUNCER
1½ oz. Old Mr. Boston
    Dry Gin
½ oz. Absinthe Substitute
Pour into old-fashioned glass over ice cubes. Stir.

MONTREAL GIN SOUR
1 oz. Old Mr. Boston Dry Gin
1 oz. Lemon Juice
½ Egg White
1 teaspoon Powdered Sugar
Shake with ice and strain into sour glass. Add slice of lemon.

MONTEZUMA

1½ oz. Gavilan Tequila
1 oz. Madeira
1 Egg Yolk
½ cup Crushed Ice
Mix in blender at low speed and serve in champagne glass.

MOONLIGHT

2 oz. Apple Brandy
Juice 1 Lemon
1 teaspoon Powdered Sugar
Shake with ice and strain into old-fashioned glass over ice cubes.

MOON QUAKE SHAKE

1½ oz. Old Mr. Boston
    Rum (Dark)
1 oz. Old Mr. Boston
    Coffee Flavored Brandy
1 tablespoon Lemon Juice
Shake with ice and strain into cocktail glass.

MORNING COCKTAIL

1 oz. Old Mr. Boston
    Five Star Brandy
1 oz. Dry Vermouth
¼ teaspoon Old Mr. Boston
    Triple Sec
¼ teaspoon Maraschino
¼ teaspoon Absinthe
    Substitute
2 dashes Orange Bitters
Stir with ice and strain into cocktail glass. Serve with a cherry.

MORNING GLORY FIZZ

Juice ½ Lemon or 1 Lime
1 teaspoon Powdered Sugar
1 Egg White
½ teaspoon Absinthe
    Substitute
2 oz. Desmond & Duff
    Scotch Whisky
Shake with ice and strain into highball glass over two cubes of ice. Fill with carbonated water and stir.

MORRO

1 oz. Old Mr. Boston Dry Gin
½ oz. Old Mr. Boston
    Rum (Dark)
1 tablespoon Pineapple Juice
1 tablespoon Lime Juice
½ teaspoon Powdered Sugar
Shake with ice and strain into sugar-rimmed old-fashioned glass over ice cubes.

MOSCOW MULE
Into a copper mug, pour:
1½ oz. Old Mr. Boston
   Vodka
Juice ½ Lime
*Add ice cubes and fill with
ginger beer. Drop lime wedge
in mug to decorate.*

MOULIN ROUGE COCKTAIL
1½ oz. Old Mr. Boston
   Sloe Gin
¾ oz. Sweet Vermouth
1 dash Bitters
*Stir with ice and strain into
cocktail glass.*

MOUNTAIN COCKTAIL
1 Egg White
¼ teaspoon Lemon Juice
¼ teaspoon Dry Vermouth
¼ teaspoon Sweet Vermouth
1½ oz. Old Thompson
   Blended Whiskey
*Shake with ice and strain into
cocktail glass.*

MULLED CLARET
Into a metal mug put:
1 lump Sugar
Juice ½ Lemon
1 dash Bitters
1 teaspoon Mixed Cinnamon
   and Nutmeg
5 oz. Claret
*Heat poker red hot and hold
in liquid until boiling and
serve.*

NAPOLEON COCKTAIL
2 oz. Old Mr. Boston Dry Gin
½ teaspoon Curaçao
½ teaspoon Dubonnet
Stir with ice and strain into cocktail glass.

NARRAGANSETT
1½ oz. Old Kentucky Tavern
  Bourbon Whiskey
1 oz. Sweet Vermouth
1 dash Old Mr. Boston
  Anisette
Stir in old-fashioned glass with ice cubes. Add a twist of lemon peel.

NEGRONI
¾ oz. Old Mr. Boston
  Dry Gin
¾ oz. Campari
¾ oz. Sweet or Dry
  Vermouth
Stir with ice and strain into cocktail glass, or into old-fashioned glass over ice cubes, with or without a splash of carbonated water. Add twist of lemon peel.

NETHERLAND
1 oz. Old Mr. Boston
  Five Star Brandy
1 oz. Old Mr. Boston
  Triple Sec
1 dash Orange Bitters
Stir in old-fashioned glass with ice cubes.

NEVADA COCKTAIL
1½ oz. Old Mr. Boston Rum
1 oz. Grapefruit Juice
Juice 1 Lime
1 dash Bitters
3 teaspoons Powdered Sugar
Shake with ice and strain into cocktail glass.

NEVINS
1½ oz. Old Kentucky Tavern
  Bourbon Whiskey
1½ teaspoons Old Mr. Boston
  Apricot Flavored
  Brandy
1 tablespoon Grapefruit Juice
1½ teaspoons Lemon Juice
1 dash Bitters
Shake with ice and strain into cocktail glass.

NEW ORLEANS BUCK
1½ oz. Old Mr. Boston Rum
1 oz. Orange Juice
½ oz. Lemon Juice
Shake all ingredients with ice and strain into collins glass over ice cubes. Fill with ginger ale and stir.

NEW ORLEANS GIN FIZZ

Juice ½ Lemon
Juice ½ Lime (optional)
1 teaspoon Powdered Sugar
1 Egg White
2 oz. Old Mr. Boston Dry Gin
1 tablespoon Sweet Cream
½ teaspoon Orange Flower
    Water

Shake with ice and strain into highball glass with two cubes of ice. Fill with carbonated water and stir.

NEW YORK COCKTAIL

Juice 1 Lime or ½ Lemon
1 teaspoon Powdered Sugar
1½ oz. Old Thompson
    Blended Whiskey
½ teaspoon Grenadine
Shake with ice and strain into cocktail glass. Add twist of lemon peel.

NEW YORK SOUR

Juice ½ Lemon
1 teaspoon Powdered Sugar
2 oz. Old Thompson
    Blended Whiskey
Shake with ice and strain into sour glass, leaving about ½ inch on which to float claret. Decorate with a half-slice lemon and a cherry.

NIGHT CAP

2 oz. Old Mr. Boston Rum
1 teaspoon Powdered Sugar
Add enough warm milk to fill a Tom-and-Jerry mug and stir. Sprinkle a little nutmeg on top.

NIGHTMARE

1½ oz. Old Mr. Boston Dry
    Gin
½ oz. Madeira
½ oz. Old Mr. Boston
    Wild Cherry Flavored
    Brandy
1 teaspoon Orange Juice
Shake with ice and strain into cocktail glass.

NINOTCHKA COCKTAIL

1½ oz. Old Mr. Boston
    Vodka
½ oz. Old Mr. Boston
    Crème de Cacao (White)
1 tablespoon Lemon Juice
Shake with ice and strain into cocktail glass.

NORTH POLE COCKTAIL

1 Egg White
½ oz. Lemon Juice
½ oz. Maraschino
1 oz. Old Mr. Boston Dry Gin
Shake with ice and strain into cocktail glass. Top with whipped cream.

OLD FASHIONED COCKTAIL

Into an old-fashioned glass put a small cube of sugar, a dash of Angostura bitters, a teaspoon of water and muddle well. Add 2 oz. Old Thompson Blended Whiskey. Stir. Add twist of lemon peel and ice cubes. Decorate with slice of orange, lemon, and a cherry. Serve with a swizzle stick.

OLD PAL COCKTAIL

½ oz. Grenadine
½ oz. Sweet Vermouth
1¼ oz. Old Thompson
    Blended Whiskey
Stir with ice and strain into cocktail glass.

OLYMPIC COCKTAIL

¾ oz. Orange Juice
¾ oz. Old Mr. Boston
    Triple Sec
¾ oz. Old Mr. Boston
    Five Star Brandy
Shake with ice and strain into cocktail glass.

OPAL COCKTAIL

1 oz. Old Mr. Boston Dry Gin
½ oz. Old Mr. Boston
    Triple Sec
1 tablespoon Orange Juice
¼ teaspoon Powdered Sugar
½ teaspoon Orange Flower
    Water
Shake with ice and strain into cocktail glass.

OPENING COCKTAIL

½ oz. Grenadine
½ oz. Sweet Vermouth
1½ oz. Old Thompson
    Blended Whiskey
Stir with ice and strain into cocktail glass.

OPERA COCKTAIL

1 tablespoon Maraschino
½ oz. Dubonnet
1½ oz. Old Mr. Boston
    Dry Gin
Stir with ice and strain into cocktail glass.

ORANGEADE

Juice 2 Oranges
1 teaspoon Powdered Sugar
Mix in collins glass. Add ice cubes and enough water to fill glass and stir. Decorate with slices of orange and lemon, and two cherries. Serve with straws.

OLD Mr. BOSTON

ORANGE BLOSSOM COCKTAIL

1 oz. Old Mr. Boston Dry Gin
1 oz. Orange Juice
¼ teaspoon Powdered Sugar
Shake with ice and strain into cocktail glass.

ORANGE BUCK

1½ oz. Old Mr. Boston Dry Gin
1 oz. Orange Juice
1 tablespoon Lime Juice
Shake with ice and strain into highball glass over ice cubes. Fill with ginger ale and stir.

ORANGE OASIS

1½ oz. Old Mr. Boston Dry Gin
½ oz. Old Mr. Boston Wild Cherry Flavored Brandy
4 oz. Orange Juice
Shake with ice and strain into highball glass over ice cubes. Fill with ginger ale and stir.

ORANGE SMILE

1 whole Egg
Juice 1 Large Orange
1 tablespoon Raspberry Syrup or Grenadine
Shake with ice and strain into stem goblet.

ORIENTAL COCKTAIL

1 oz. Old Thompson Blended Whiskey
½ oz. Sweet Vermouth
½ oz. Old Mr. Boston Triple Sec
Juice ½ Lime
Shake with ice and strain into cocktail glass.

OUTRIGGER

1 oz. Old Mr. Boston Peach Flavored Brandy
1 oz. Old Mr. Boston Lime Vodka
1 oz. Pineapple Juice
Shake with ice and strain into old-fashioned glass over ice cubes.

P

PADDY COCKTAIL
1½ oz. Irish Whisky
1½ oz. Sweet Vermouth
1 dash Bitters
Stir with ice and strain into cocktail glass.

PAISLEY MARTINI
2 oz. Old Mr. Boston Dry Gin
½ oz. Dry Vermouth
1 teaspoon Desmond & Duff Scotch Whisky
Stir in old-fashioned glass over ice cubes. Add twist of lemon peel.

PALL MALL
1½ oz. Old Mr. Boston Dry Gin
½ oz. Sweet Vermouth
½ oz. Dry Vermouth
½ oz. Old Mr. Boston Crème de Menthe (White)
Stir in old-fashioned glass over ice cubes.

PALM BEACH COCKTAIL
1½ oz. Old Mr. Boston Dry Gin
1½ teaspoons Sweet Vermouth
1½ teaspoons Grapefruit Juice
Shake with ice and strain into cocktail glass.

PALMER COCKTAIL
2 oz. Old Thompson Blended Whiskey
1 dash Bitters
½ teaspoon Lemon Juice
Stir with ice and strain into cocktail glass.

PALMETTO COCKTAIL
1½ oz. Old Mr. Boston Rum
1½ oz. Dry Vermouth
2 dashes Bitters
Stir with ice and strain into cocktail glass.

PANAMA COCKTAIL
1 oz. Old Mr. Boston Crème de Cacao
1 oz. Sweet Cream
1 oz. Old Mr. Boston Five Star Brandy
Shake with ice and strain into cocktail glass.

PAPAYA SLING
1½ oz. Old Mr. Boston Dry Gin
1 dash Bitters
Juice 1 Lime
1 tablespoon Papaya Syrup
Shake with ice and strain into collins glass over ice cubes. Fill with carbonated water and stir. Add a pineapple stick.

PARADISE COCKTAIL

1 oz. Old Mr. Boston
    Apricot Flavored Brandy
¾ oz. Old Mr. Boston
    Dry Gin
Juice ¼ Orange
Shake with ice and strain into cocktail glass.

PARISIAN

1 oz. Old Mr. Boston Dry Gin
1 oz. Dry Vermouth
½ oz. Mr. Boston
    Crème de Cassis
Shake with ice and strain into cocktail glass.

PARISIAN BLONDE COCKTAIL

¾ oz. Sweet Cream
¾ oz. Old Mr. Boston
    Triple Sec
¾ oz. Jamaica Rum
Shake with ice and strain into cocktail glass.

PARK AVENUE

1½ oz. Old Mr. Boston
    Dry Gin
¾ oz. Sweet Vermouth
1 tablespoon Pineapple Juice
Stir with ice and strain into cocktail glass.

PASSION DAIQUIRI COCKTAIL

1½ oz. Old Mr. Boston Rum
Juice 1 Lime
1 teaspooon Powdered Sugar
1 tablespoon Passion Fruit
    Juice
Shake with ice and strain into cocktail glass.

PEACH BLOSSOM

1 teaspoon Lemon Juice
½ teaspoon Powdered Sugar
2 oz. Old Mr. Boston Dry Gin
½ Peach
Shake with ice and strain into highball glass over ice cubes. Fill with carbonated water and stir.

PEACH BLOW FIZZ

Juice ½ Lemon
½ teaspoon Powdered Sugar
1 oz. Sweet Cream
2 oz. Old Mr. Boston Dry Gin
¼ Peach
Shake with ice and strain into highball glass over ice cubes. Fill with carbonated water and stir.

OLD Mr. BOSTON

PEACH BUNNY

¾ oz. Old Mr. Boston Peach Flavored Brandy
¾ oz. Old Mr. Boston Crème de Cacao (White)
¾ oz. Light Sweet Cream
Shake well with ice and strain into cocktail glass.

PEACH SANGAREE

Put 2 oz. Old Mr. Boston Peach Flavored Brandy in highball glass with ice cubes. Fill glass with carbonated water, leaving enough room on which to float a teaspoon Port. Stir and float wine on top. Sprinkle lightly with nutmeg.

PEGGY COCKTAIL

¾ oz. Dry Vermouth
1½ oz. Old Mr. Boston Dry Gin
¼ teaspoon Absinthe Substitute
¼ teaspoon Dubonnet
Stir with ice and strain into cocktail glass.

PENDENNIS TODDY

Muddle a lump of sugar with one teaspoon of water, in sour glass. Fill with ice, add 2 oz. Old Kentucky Tavern Bourbon *and stir. Decorate with two slices of lemon.*

PEPPERMINT ICEBERG

Pour 2 oz. Mr. Boston Peppermint Schnapps into old-fashioned glass over ice cubes. Stir and serve with a peppermint-candy swizzle stick.

PEPPERMINT PATTIE

1 oz. Old Mr. Boston Crème de Cacao (White)
1 oz. Old Mr. Boston Crème de Menthe (White)
Shake with ice and strain into old-fashioned glass over ice cubes.

PEPPERMINT STICK

1 oz. Mr. Boston Peppermint Schnapps
1½ oz. Mr. Boston Crème de Cacao (White)
1 oz. Sweet Cream
Shake with ice and strain into champagne glass.

PERFECT COCKTAIL

1½ teaspoons Dry Vermouth
1½ teaspoons Sweet Vermouth
1½ oz. Old Mr. Boston Dry Gin
1 dash Bitters
Stir with ice and strain into cocktail glass.

PETER PAN COCKTAIL

2 dashes Bitters
¾ oz. Orange Juice
¾ oz. Dry Vermouth
¾ oz. Old Mr. Boston Dry Gin
Shake with ice and strain into cocktail glass.

PHOEBE SNOW COCKTAIL

1½ oz. Dubonnet
1½ oz. Old Mr. Boston
  Five Star Brandy
½ teaspoon Absinthe
  Substitute

Stir with ice and strain into cocktail glass.

PICCADILLY COCKTAIL

¾ oz. Dry Vermouth
1½ oz. Old Mr. Boston
  Dry Gin
¼ teaspoon Absinthe
  Substitute
¼ teaspoon Grenadine

Stir with ice and strain into cocktail glass.

PICON COCKTAIL

See Amer Picon Cocktail on page 5.

PIKE'S PEAK COOLER

Juice ½ Lemon
1 teaspoon Powdered Sugar
1 Whole Egg

Shake with ice and strain into collins glass with cracked ice. Fill with hard cider and stir. Insert spiral of orange or lemon peel (or both) and dangle end over rim of glass.

PINA COLADA

3 oz. Old Mr. Boston Rum
3 tablespoons Coconut Milk
3 tablespoons Crushed
  Pineapple

Place in blender with two cups of crushed ice and blend at high speed for a short time. Strain into collins glass and serve with straw.

PINEAPPLE COCKTAIL

¾ oz. Pineapple Juice
1½ oz. Old Mr. Boston Rum
½ teaspoon Lemon Juice

Shake with ice and strain into cocktail glass.

PINEAPPLE COOLER

Into collins glass put:
2 oz. Pineapple Juice
½ teaspoon Powdered Sugar
2 oz. Carbonated Water

Stir. Add ice cubes and 2 oz. Dry White Wine. Fill with carbonated water and stir again. Insert spiral of orange or lemon peel (or both) and dangle end over rim of glass.

PINEAPPLE FIZZ

1 oz. Pineapple Juice
½ teaspoon Powdered Sugar
2 oz. Old Mr. Boston Rum

Shake with ice and strain into highball glass over two cubes of ice. Fill with carbonated water and stir.

PING-PONG COCKTAIL

Juice ¼ Lemon
1 Egg White
2 oz. Mr. Boston Sloe Gin
Shake with ice and strain into cocktail glass.

PINK CREOLE

1½ oz. Old Mr. Boston Rum
1 tablespoon Lime Juice
1 teaspoon Grenadine
1 teaspoon Sweet Cream
Shake with ice and strain into cocktail glass. Add a black cherry soaked in rum.

PINK GIN

See Gin and Bitters recipe on page 62.

PINK LADY COCKTAIL

1 Egg White
1 teaspoon Grenadine
1 teaspoon Sweet Cream
1½ oz. Old Mr. Boston
    Dry Gin
Shake with ice and strain into cocktail glass.

PINK PUSSY CAT

Into a highball glass almost filled with ice put 1½ oz. Old Mr. Boston Vodka or Dry Gin. Fill balance of glass with pineapple or grapefruit juice. Add dash of grenadine for color and stir.

PINK ROSE FIZZ

Juice ½ Lemon
1 teaspoon Powdered Sugar
1 Egg White
2 teaspoons Sweet Cream
2 oz. Old Mr. Boston Dry Gin
Shake with ice and strain into highball glass over two cubes of ice. Fill with carbonated water and stir.

PINK SQUIRREL COCKTAIL

1 oz. Mr. Boston
    Crème de Noyaux
1 tablespoon Old Mr. Boston
    Crème de Cacao (White)
1 tablespoon Lt. Sweet Cream
Shake with ice and strain into cocktail glass.

PLAIN VERMOUTH COCKTAIL

See Vermouth Cocktail page 156.

PLANTER'S COCKTAIL

Juice ¼ Lemon
½ teaspoon Powdered Sugar
1½ oz. Jamaica Rum
Shake with ice and strain into cocktail glass.

PLANTER'S PUNCH NO. 1

Juice 2 Limes
2 teaspoons Powdered Sugar
2 oz. Carbonated Water
Mix in a collins glass, add ice cubes and stir until glass is frosted. Add two dashes Bitters, 2½ oz. Old Mr. Boston Rum. Stir and decorate with slices of lemon, orange, pineapple, and a cherry. Serve with a straw.

PLANTER'S PUNCH NO. 2

Juice 1 Lime
Juice ½ Lemon
Juice ½ Orange
1 teaspoon Pineapple Juice
2 oz. Old Mr. Boston Rum
Pour into collins glass, well filled with ice. Stir until glass is frosted. Then add 1 oz. Jamaica Rum, stir, and top with 2 dashes Old Mr. Boston Triple Sec. Decorate with slices of orange, lemon, pineapple, and a cherry, also sprig of mint dipped in powdered sugar. Serve with a straw.

PLAZA COCKTAIL

¾ oz. Sweet Vermouth
¾ oz. Dry Vermouth
¾ oz. Old Mr. Boston
    Dry Gin
Shake with ice and strain into cocktail glass. Add a strip of pineapple.

POKER COCKTAIL

1½ oz. Sweet Vermouth
1½ oz. Old Mr. Boston Rum
Stir with ice and strain into cocktail glass.

POLLYANNA COCKTAIL

Muddle 3 slices of orange and 3 slices of pineapple with:
2 oz. Old Mr. Boston Dry Gin
½ oz. Sweet Vermouth
½ teaspoon Grenadine
Shake with ice and strain into cocktail glass.

POLO COCKTAIL

1 tablespoon Lemon Juice
1 tablespoon Orange Juice
1 oz. Old Mr. Boston Dry Gin
Shake with ice and strain into cocktail glass.

POLONAISE

1½ oz. Old Mr. Boston
    Five Star Brandy
1 tablespoon Old Mr. Boston
    Blackberry Flavored
    Brandy
½ oz. Dry Sherry
1 dash Lemon Juice
Shake with ice and strain into old-fashioned glass over ice cubes.

POLYNESIAN COCKTAIL

1½ oz. Old Mr. Boston
    Vodka
¾ oz. Old Mr. Boston Wild
    Cherry Flavored Brandy
Juice 1 Lime
Rub rim of cocktail glass with lime and dip into powdered sugar. Shake above ingredients with ice and strain into prepared glass.

POMPANO

1 oz. Old Mr. Boston Dry Gin
½ oz. Dry Vermouth
1 oz. Grapefruit Juice
Shake with ice and strain into cocktail glass.

POOP DECK COCKTAIL

1 oz. Old Mr. Boston
    Five Star Brandy
1 oz. Port
1 tablespoon Old Mr. Boston
    Blackberry Flavored
    Brandy
Shake with ice and strain into cocktail glass.

POPPY COCKTAIL

¾ oz. Old Mr. Boston
    Crème de Cacao (White)
1½ oz. Old Mr. Boston
    Dry Gin
Shake with ice and strain into cocktail glass.

PORT AND STARBOARD

1 tablespoon Grenadine
½ oz. Old Mr. Boston
    Crème de Menthe (Green)
Pour carefully into pousse-café glass, so that crème de menthe floats on grenadine.

PORT MILK PUNCH

1 teaspoon Powdered Sugar
2 oz. Port
1 cup Milk
Shake with ice and strain into collins glass. Sprinkle nutmeg on top.

PORT WINE COBBLER

Dissolve 1 teaspoon powdered sugar in 2 oz. carbonated water; then fill goblet with shaved ice and add 3 oz. Port. Stir and decorate with fruits in season. Serve with straws.

PORT WINE COCKTAIL

2½ oz. Port
½ teaspoon Old Mr. Boston
    Five Star Brandy
Stir with ice and strain into cocktail glass.

PORT WINE EGGNOG

1 Whole Egg
1 teaspoon Powdered Sugar
3 oz. Port
6 oz. Milk
Shake well with ice and strain into collins glass. Sprinkle nutmeg on top.

OLD Mr. BOSTON

PORT WINE FLIP

1 Whole Egg
1 teaspoon Powdered Sugar
1½ oz. Port
2 teaspoons Sweet Cream
(if desired)
Shake with ice and strain into flip glass. Sprinkle a little nutmeg on top.

PORT WINE NEGUS

½ lump Sugar
2 oz. Port
Pour into hot whisky glass, fill with hot water and stir. Sprinkle nutmeg on top.

PORT WINE SANGAREE

Dissolve ½ teaspoon powdered sugar in 1 teaspoon water in highball glass. Add 2 oz. Port and ice cubes. Fill with carbonated water leaving enough room on which to float a tablespoon of Brandy. Stir. Float brandy on top. Sprinkle with nutmeg.

POUSSE CAFÉ

1/6 Grenadine
1/6 Chartreuse (Yellow)
1/6 Mr. Boston Crème de Cassis
1/6 Mr. Boston Crème de Menthe (White)
1/6 Chartreuse (Green)
1/6 Mr. Boston Five Star Brandy
Pour carefully, in order given, into pousse-café glass so that each ingredient floats on preceding one.
(For other Pousse Café recipes, see Index on page 206.)

POUSSE L'AMOUR

1 tablespoon Maraschino
1 Egg Yolk
½ oz. Benedictine
½ oz. Old Mr. Boston Five Star Brandy
Pour carefully, in order given, into 2 oz. sherry glass, so that each ingredient floats on preceding one.

PRADO

1½ oz. Gavilan Tequila
¾ oz. Lemon Juice
1 tablespoon Maraschino
½ Egg White
1 teaspoon Grenadine
Shake with ice and strain into sour glass. Add a slice of lime and a cherry.

PRAIRIE CHICKEN

1 oz. Old Mr. Boston Dry Gin
1 Whole Egg
Pepper and Salt
Open egg without breaking the yolk and put in wine glass. Pour gin on top. Add pepper and salt.

PRAIRIE OYSTER COCKTAIL

1 oz. Old Mr. Boston Five Star Brandy
1 tablespoon Worchestershire Sauce
1 teaspoon Tomato Catsup
1 tablespoon Vinegar
1 pinch Pepper
Shake with ice and strain into old-fashioned glass over two ice cubes. Place an egg yolk on top without breaking it. Add a dash of cayenne pepper.

OLD Mr. BOSTON

PREAKNESS COCKTAIL

¾ oz. Sweet Vermouth
1½ oz. Old Thompson
   Blended Whiskey
1 dash Bitters
½ teaspoon Benedictine
Stir with ice and strain into cocktail glass. Add twist of lemon peel.

PRESTO COCKTAIL

1 tablespoon Orange Juice
½ oz. Sweet Vermouth
1½ oz. Old Mr. Boston
   Five Star Brandy
¼ teaspoon Absinthe
   Substitute
Shake with ice and strain into cocktail glass.

PRINCE'S SMILE COCKTAIL

½ oz. Old Mr. Boston
   Apricot Flavored Brandy
½ oz. Apple Brandy
1 oz. Old Mr. Boston Dry Gin
¼ teaspoon Lemon Juice
Shake with ice and strain into cocktail glass.

PRINCESS POUSSE CAFÉ

¾ oz. Old Mr. Boston
   Apricot Flavored Brandy
1½ teaspoons Sweet Cream
Pour cream carefully on top of brandy, so that it does not mix. Use pousse-café glass.

PRINCETON COCKTAIL

1 oz. Old Mr. Boston Dry
   Gin
1 oz. Dry Vermouth
Juice ½ Lime
Stir with ice and strain into cocktail glass.

PUERTO APPLE

1½ oz. Applejack
¾ oz. Old Mr. Boston Rum
1 tablespoon Lime Juice
1 oz. Orgeat Syrup
Shake with ice and strain into old-fashioned glass over ice cubes. Decorate with a slice of lime.

PUNCHES

See Index on page 206 for complete list of Punch recipes.

PURPLE MASK

1 oz. Old Mr. Boston Vodka
1 oz. Grape Juice
½ oz. Old Mr. Boston
   Crème de Cacao (White)
Shake with ice and strain into cocktail glass.

QUAKER'S COCKTAIL
¾ oz. Old Mr. Boston Rum
¾ oz. Old Mr. Boston
   Five Star Brandy
Juice ¼ Lemon
2 teaspoons Raspberry Syrup
Shake with ice and strain into cocktail glass.

QUARTER DECK COCKTAIL
⅓ oz. Sweet Sherry
1½ oz. Old Mr. Boston Rum
Juice ½ Lime
Stir with ice and strain into cocktail glass.

QUEBEC
1½ oz. Old Mr. Boston Five
   Star Canadian Whisky
½ oz. Dry Vermouth
1½ teaspoons Amer Picon
1½ teaspoons Maraschino
Shake with ice and strain into cocktail glass rimmed with sugar.

QUEEN BEE
1½ oz. Old Mr. Boston
   Lime Vodka
1 oz. Old Mr. Boston
   Coffee Flavored Brandy
½ oz. Sweet Sherry
Shake with ice and strain into cocktail glass.

QUEEN CHARLOTTE
2 oz. Claret
1 oz. Raspberry Syrup or
   Grenadine
Pour into collins glass over ice cubes. Fill with lemon soda and stir.

QUEEN ELIZABETH COCKTAIL
1½ oz. Old Mr. Boston
   Dry Gin
½ oz. Dry Vermouth
1½ teaspoons Benedictine
Stir with ice and strain into cocktail glass.

R

RACQUET CLUB COCKTAIL
1½ oz. Old Mr. Boston
    Dry Gin
¾ oz. Dry Vermouth
1 dash Orange Bitters
Stir with ice and strain into cocktail glass.

RAMOS FIZZ
Juice ½ Lemon
1 Egg White
1 teaspoon Powdered Sugar
2 oz. Old Mr. Boston Dry Gin
1 tablespoon Sweet Cream
½ teaspoon Orange Flower
    Water
Shake with ice and strain into highball glass over two cubes of ice. Fill with carbonated water and stir.

RATTLESNAKE COCKTAIL
1½ oz. Old Thompson
    Blended Whiskey
1 Egg White
1 teaspoon Lemon Juice
½ teaspoon Powdered Sugar
¼ teaspoon Absinthe
    Substitute
Shake with ice and strain into cocktail glass.

REBEL CHARGE
1 oz. Old Kentucky Tavern
    Bourbon Whiskey
½ oz. Old Mr. Boston
    Triple Sec
1 tablespoon Orange Juice
1 tablespoon Lemon Juice
½ Egg White
Shake with ice and strain into old-fashioned glass over ice cubes. Add orange slice.

RED APPLE
1 oz. Old Mr. Boston
    100 Proof Vodka
1 oz. Apple Juice
1 tablespoon Lemon Juice
1 teaspoon Grenadine
Shake with ice and strain into cocktail glass.

RED CLOUD

1½ oz. Old Mr. Boston
    Dry Gin
½ oz. Old Mr. Boston
    Apricot Flavored Brandy
1 tablespoon Lemon Juice
1 teaspoon Grenadine
*Shake with ice and strain into
cocktail glass.*

RED RAIDER

1 oz. Old Kentucky Tavern
    Bourbon Whiskey
½ oz. Old Mr. Boston
    Triple Sec
1 oz. Lemon Juice
1 dash Grenadine
*Shake with ice and strain into
cocktail glass.*

RED SWIZZLE

Make the same as Gin Swizzle (see page 64), and add one tablespoon of grenadine. If desired, rum, brandy, or whiskey may be substituted for the gin.

REFORM COCKTAIL

¾ oz. Dry Vermouth
1½ oz. Dry Sherry
1 dash Orange Bitters
*Stir with ice and strain into
cocktail glass. Serve with a
cherry.*

REMSEN COOLER

Into collins glass, put ½ teaspoon powdered sugar and 2 oz. carbonated water. Stir. Add ice cubes and 2 oz. Old Mr. Boston Dry Gin. Fill with carbonated water and ginger ale and stir again. Insert spiral of orange or lemon peel (or both) and dangle end over rim of glass.

RENAISSANCE COCKTAIL

1½ oz. Old Mr. Boston
    Dry Gin
½ oz. Dry Sherry
1 tablespoon Sweet Cream
*Shake with ice and strain into
cocktail glass. Sprinkle with
nutmeg.*

RESOLUTE COCKTAIL

Juice ¼ Lemon
½ oz. Old Mr. Boston
    Apricot Flavored Brandy
1 oz. Old Mr. Boston Dry Gin
*Shake with ice and strain into
cocktail glass.*

RHINE WINE CUP

4 teaspoons Powdered Sugar
6 oz. Carbonated Water
1 oz. Mr. Boston Triple Sec
2 oz. Old Mr. Boston
    Five Star Brandy
Mix ingredients and pour into large glass pitcher over cubes of ice. Add 1 pt. Rhine Wine. Stir and decorate with as many fruits as available. Insert rind of cucumber on each side of pitcher. Top with mint sprigs. Serve in claret glasses.

RICKIES

See Index on page 207 for complete list of Rickey recipes.

ROAD RUNNER

1 oz. Old Mr. Boston Vodka
½ oz. Amaretto Di Saronno
½ oz. Coconut Cream
Mix in blender with ½ scoop of crushed ice for 15 seconds. Rim edge of a chilled 4½ oz. champagne glass with a slice of orange. Dip rim in a sugar and nutmeg mixture. Pour cocktail into the prepared glass. Top with a dash of nutmeg.

ROB ROY COCKTAIL

¾ oz. Sweet Vermouth
1½ oz. Desmond & Duff
    Scotch Whisky
Stir with ice and strain into cocktail glass.

ROBERT E. LEE COOLER

Into collins glass, put:
Juice ½ Lime
½ teaspoon Powdered Sugar
2 oz. Carbonated Water
Stir. Add ice cubes and:
¼ teaspoon Absinthe
    Substitute
2 oz. Old Mr. Boston Dry Gin
Fill with ginger ale and stir again. Add spiral of orange or lemon peel (or both) and dangle end over rim of glass.

ROBIN'S NEST

1 oz. Old Mr. Boston Vodka
1 oz. Cranberry Juice
½ oz. Old Mr. Boston
    Crème de Cacao (White)
Shake with ice and strain into cocktail glass.

ROBSON COCKTAIL

2 teaspoons Lemon Juice
1 tablespoon Orange Juice
1½ teaspoons Grenadine
1 oz. Jamaica Rum
Shake with ice and strain into cocktail glass.

ROCK & RYE COCKTAIL

1 oz. Old Mr. Boston
    Rock & Rye
1 oz. White Port
1½ teaspoons Dry Vermouth
Stir with ice and strain into cocktail glass.

ROCK & RYE COOLER

1 oz. Old Mr. Boston
    Rock & Rye
1½ oz. Old Mr. Boston
    Vodka
1 tablespoon Lime Juice
Shake with ice and strain into collins glass over ice cubes. Fill with bitter-lemon soda and stir.

ROCOCO

1 oz. Old Mr. Boston
    Cherry Vodka
1 oz. Orange Juice
½ oz. Old Mr. Boston
    Triple Sec
Shake with ice and strain into cocktail glass.

ROLLS-ROYCE COCKTAIL
½ oz. Dry Vermouth
½ oz. Sweet Vermouth
1½ oz. Old Mr. Boston
　　Dry Gin
¼ teaspoon Benedictine
Stir with ice and strain into cocktail glass.

RORY O'MORE
¾ oz. Sweet Vermouth
1½ oz. Irish Whisky
1 dash Orange Bitters
Stir with ice and strain into cocktail glass.

ROSE COCKTAIL (ENGLISH)
½ oz. Old Mr. Boston
　　Apricot Flavored Brandy
½ oz. Dry Vermouth
1 oz. Old Mr. Boston
　　Dry Gin
½ teaspoon Lemon Juice
1 teaspoon Grenadine
Moisten rim of cocktail glass with lemon juice and dip into powdered sugar. Shake above ingredients with ice and strain into prepared glass.

ROSE COCKTAIL (FRENCH)
½ oz. Old Mr. Boston
　　Wild Cherry Flavored
　　Brandy
½ oz. Dry Vermouth
1½ oz. Old Mr. Boston
　　Dry Gin
Stir with ice and strain into cocktail glass.

ROSELYN COCKTAIL
¾ oz. Dry Vermouth
1½ oz. Old Mr. Boston
　　Dry Gin
½ teaspoon Grenadine
Stir with ice and strain into cocktail glass. Add a twist of lemon peel.

ROSITA
1 oz. Gavilan Tequila
½ oz. Dry Vermouth
½ oz. Sweet Vermouth
1 oz. Campari
Stir in old-fashioned glass with cracked ice. Add a twist of lemon peel and serve with short straws.

ROYAL CLOVER CLUB COCKTAIL
Juice 1 Lime
1 tablespoon Grenadine
1 Egg Yolk
1½ oz. Old Mr. Boston
　　Dry Gin
Shake with ice and strain into flip glass.

ROYAL COCKTAIL

1 Whole Egg
Juice ½ Lemon
½ teaspoon Powdered Sugar
1½ oz. Old Mr. Boston
   Dry Gin
*Shake with ice and strain into
flip glass.*

ROYAL GIN FIZZ

Juice ½ Lemon
1 teaspoon Powdered Sugar
2 oz. Old Mr. Boston Dry Gin
1 Whole Egg
*Shake with ice and strain into
highball glass with two cubes
of ice. Fill with carbonated
water and stir.*

ROYAL PURPLE PUNCH

*Pour two large bottles (750 ml
size) claret and two large bottles
ginger ale over ice cubes in
punch bowl. Stir well. Float thin
slices of lemon studded with
cloves on top. Serve in punch
glasses.*

ROYAL SMILE COCKTAIL

Juice ¼ Lemon
1 teaspoon Grenadine
½ oz. Old Mr. Boston
   Dry Gin
1 oz. Apple Brandy
*Stir with ice and strain into
cocktail glass.*

RUBY FIZZ

Juice ½ Lemon
1 teaspoon Powdered Sugar
1 Egg White
1 teaspoon Grenadine
2 oz. Old Mr. Boston
   Sloe Gin
*Shake with ice and strain into
highball glass over two cubes
of ice. Fill with carbonated
water and stir.*

RUM COBBLER

*In a goblet, dissolve 1 tea-
spoon powdered sugar in 2
oz. carbonated water. Fill
goblet with shaved ice, and
add 2 oz. Old Mr. Boston
Rum. Stir and decorate with
fruits in season. Serve with a
straw.*

RUM COLA

*See Cuba Libra recipe on
page 45.*

RUM COLLINS

Juice 1 Lime
1 teaspoon Powdered Sugar
2 oz. Old Mr. Boston Rum
*Shake with ice and strain into
collins glass. Add several
cubes of ice, fill with carbonated water, and stir. Decorate with slice of lemon and
a cherry. Serve with a straw.*

OLD Mr. BOSTON

RUM COOLER

In collins glass, dissolve ½ teaspoon powdered sugar in 2 oz. carbonated water. Stir. Fill glass with ice and add 2 oz. Old Mr. Boston Rum. Fill with carbonated water or ginger ale and stir again. Insert spiral of orange or lemon peel (or both) and dangle end over rim of glass.

RUM DAISY

Juice ½ Lemon
½ teaspoon Powdered Sugar
1 teaspoon Raspberry Syrup
    or Grenadine
2 oz. Old Mr. Boston Rum
Shake with ice and strain into stein or metal cup. Add an ice cube and decorate with fruit.

RUM DUBONNET

1½ oz. Old Mr. Boston Rum
1½ teaspoons Dubonnet
1 teaspoon Lemon Juice
Shake with ice and strain into cocktail glass.

RUM EGGNOG

1 Whole Egg
1 teaspoon Powdered Sugar
2 oz. Old Mr. Boston Rum
6 oz. Milk
Shake with ice and strain into collins glass. Sprinkle nutmeg on top.

RUM FIX

Juice ½ Lemon or 1 Lime
1 teaspoon Powdered Sugar
1 teaspoon Water
Stir together in a highball glass and fill glass with ice. Add 2½ oz. Old Mr. Boston Rum. Stir and add slice of lemon. Serve with a straw.

RUM HIGHBALL

Pour 2 oz. Old Mr. Boston Rum in highball glass over ice cubes and fill with ginger ale or carbonated water. Add twist of lemon peel, if desired, and stir.

RUM OLD FASHIONED

½ teaspoon Powdered Sugar
1 dash Bitters
1 teaspoon Water
1½ oz. Old Mr. Boston
    Light Rum
1 teaspoon 151 Proof Rum
Stir sugar, bitters, and water in old-fashioned glass. When sugar is dissolved, add ice cubes and golden rum. Add twist of lime peel and float the 151-proof rum on top.

RUM MILK PUNCH

1 teaspoon Powdered Sugar
2 oz. Old Mr. Boston Rum
1 cup Milk
Shake with ice, strain into collins glass and sprinkle nutmeg on top.

RUM RICKEY

Juice ½ Lime
1½ oz. Old Mr. Boston Rum
Pour into highball glass over ice cubes and fill with carbonated water and ice cubes. Stir. Add wedge of lime.

RUM RUNNER

1½ oz. Old Mr. Boston
    Dry Gin
Juice 1 Lime
1 oz. Pineapple Juice
1 teaspoon Sugar
1 dash Peychaud Bitters
Shake with ice and strain over ice cubes in an old-fashioned glass rimmed with salt.

RUM SCREWDRIVER

1½ oz. Old Mr. Boston Rum
5 oz. Orange Juice
Combine ingredients in highball glass with ice cubes.

RUM SOUR

Juice ½ Lemon
½ teaspoon Powdered Sugar
2 oz. Old Mr. Boston Rum
Shake with ice and strain into sour glass. Decorate with a half-slice of lemon and a cherry.

RUM SWIZZLE

Made same as Gin Swizzle (see page 64), substituting 2 oz. Old Mr. Boston Rum.

RUM TODDY

In old-fashioned glass dissolve ½ teaspoon powdered sugar in 2 teaspoons water. Stir and add 2 oz. Old Mr. Boston Rum and a cube of ice. Stir again and add a twist of lemon peel.

RUM TODDY (HOT)

Put lump of sugar into hot whiskey glass and fill ⅔ with boiling water. Add 2 oz. Old Mr. Boston Rum. Stir and decorate with slice of lemon. Sprinkle nutmeg on top.

RUSSIAN BEAR COCKTAIL

1 oz. Old Mr. Boston Vodka
½ oz. Old Mr. Boston
    Crème de Cacao (White)
1 tablespoon Sweet Cream
Stir with ice and strain into cocktail glass.

OLD Mr. BOSTON

RUSSIAN COCKTAIL

¾ oz. Old Mr. Boston
    Crème de Cacao (White)
¾ oz. Old Mr. Boston
    Dry Gin
¾ oz. Old Mr. Boston Vodka
Shake with ice and strain into cocktail glass.

RUSTY NAIL

¾ oz. Desmond & Duff
    Scotch Whisky
¼ oz. Drambuie
Serve in old-fashioned glass with ice cubes. Float Drambuie on top.

RYE HIGHBALL

Put 2 oz. Rye Whiskey in highball glass over ice cubes and fill with ginger ale or carbonated water and ice cubes. Add twist of lemon peel, if desired, and stir.

RYE WHISKEY COCKTAIL

1 dash Bitters
1 teaspoon Powdered Sugar
2 oz. Rye Whiskey
Shake with ice and strain into cocktail glass. Serve with a cherry.

S

St. Charles Punch

1 oz. Old Mr. Boston
  Five Star Brandy
½ oz. Old Mr. Boston
  Triple Sec
3 oz. Port
Juice 1 Lemon
1 teaspoon Sugar
*Shake all ingredients with ice
except Port. Strain into collins
glass with ice. Top with port.
Add slice of lemon and a
cherry.*

St. Patrick's Day Cocktail

¾ oz. Old Mr. Boston
  Crème de Menthe (Green)
¾ oz. Chartreuse (Green)
¾ oz. Irish Whisky
1 dash Bitters
*Stir with ice and strain into
cocktail glass.*

Salty Dog

1½ oz. Old Mr. Boston
  Dry Gin
5 oz. Grapefruit Juice
¼ teaspoon Salt
*Pour into highball glass over
ice cubes. Stir well. (Old*

*Mr. Boston Vodka may be sub-
stituted for the Old Mr. Boston
Gin mentioned above.)*

San Francisco Cocktail

¾ oz. Old Mr. Boston
  Sloe Gin
¾ oz. Sweet Vermouth
¾ oz. Dry Vermouth
1 dash Bitters
1 dash Orange Bitters
*Shake with ice and strain into
cocktail glass. Serve with a
cherry.*

Sand-Martin Cocktail

1 teaspoon Chartreuse
  (Green)
1½ oz. Sweet Vermouth
1½ oz. Old Mr. Boston
  Dry Gin
*Stir with ice and strain into
cocktail glass.*

Sangarees

*See Index on page 208 for
complete list of Sangaree recipes.*

San Sebastian

1 oz. Old Mr. Boston Dry Gin
1½ teaspoons Old Mr.
  Boston Rum
1 tablespoon Grapefruit Juice
1½ teaspoons Old Mr.
  Boston Triple Sec
1 tablespoon Lemon Juice
*Shake with ice and strain into
cocktail glass.*

OLD Mr. BOSTON

SANTIAGO COCKTAIL

½ teaspoon Powdered Sugar
¼ teaspoon Grenadine
Juice 1 Lime
1½ oz. Old Mr. Boston Rum
Shake with ice and strain into cocktail glass.

SANTINI'S POUSSE CAFÉ

½ oz. Old Mr. Boston
    Five Star Brandy
1 tablespoon Maraschino
½ oz. Old Mr. Boston
    Triple Sec
½ oz. Old Mr. Boston
    Rum
Pour in order given into pousse-café glass carefully laying the syrup on top of the lower ring of brandy.

SARATOGA COCKTAIL

2 oz. Old Mr. Boston
    Five Star Brandy
2 dashes Bitters
1 teaspoon Lemon Juice
1 teaspoon Pineapple Juice
½ teaspoon Maraschino
Shake with ice and strain into cocktail glass.

SARONNO

1 oz. Amaretto di Saronno
1 oz. Mr. Boston Five Star
    Brandy
1 oz. Sweet Cream
Shake well with cracked ice. Strain and serve in cocktail glass.

SARONNO MIST

1½ oz. Amaretto di Saronno
Serve in an old-fashioned glass over crushed ice with a twist of lemon or a wedge of lime, if desired.

SAUCY SUE COCKTAIL

½ teaspoon Old Mr. Boston
    Apricot Flavored Brandy
½ teaspoon Absinthe
    Substitute
2 oz. Apple Brandy
Stir with ice and strain into cocktail glass.

SAUTERNE CUP

4 teaspoons Powdered Sugar
6 oz. Carbonated Water
1 tablespoon Old Mr. Boston
    Triple Sec
1 tablespoon Curaçao
2 oz. Old Mr. Boston
    Five Star Brandy
Fill large glass pitcher with ice. Add one pint of sauterne. Stir and decorate with as many fruits as available and also rind of cucumber inserted on each side of pitcher. Top with small bunch of mint sprigs. Serve in claret glass.

SAVANNAH

Juice ½ Orange
1 oz. Old Mr. Boston Dry Gin
1 dash Old Mr. Boston
    Crème de Cacao (White)
1 Egg White
Shake with ice and strain into cocktail glass.

SAXON COCKTAIL

Juice ½ Lime
½ teaspoon Grenadine
1¾ oz. Old Mr. Boston Rum
Shake with ice and strain into cocktail glass. Serve with a twist of orange peel.

SCOOTER

1 oz. Amaretto Di Saronno
1 oz. Old Mr. Boston
    Five Star Brandy
1 oz. Sweet Cream
Combine in blender or shake well with cracked ice. Strain into cocktail glass.

SCOTCH BIRD FLYER

1½ oz. Desmond & Duff
    Scotch Whisky
1 Egg Yolk
½ oz. Old Mr. Boston
    Triple Sec
½ teaspoon Powdered Sugar
1 oz. Sweet Cream
Shake with ice and strain into champagne glass.

SCOTCH BISHOP COCKTAIL

1 oz. Desmond & Duff
    Scotch Whisky
1 tablespoon Orange Juice
½ oz. Dry Vermouth
½ teaspoon Old Mr. Boston
    Triple Sec
¼ teaspoon Powdered Sugar
Shake with ice and strain into cocktail glass. Add a twist of lemon peel.

SCOTCH COOLER

2 oz. Desmond & Duff
    Scotch Whisky
3 dashes Old Mr. Boston
    Crème de Menthe (White)
Pour into highball glass over ice cubes. Fill with chilled carbonated water and stir.

SCOTCH HOLIDAY SOUR

1½ oz. Desmond & Duff
    Scotch Whisky
1 oz. Old Mr. Boston Wild
    Cherry Flavored Brandy
½ oz. Sweet Vermouth
1 oz. Lemon Juice
Shake with ice and strain into old-fashioned glass over ice cubes. Add slice of lemon.

SCOTCH MILK PUNCH

2 oz. Desmond & Duff
    Scotch Whisky
6 oz. Milk
1 teaspoon Powdered Sugar
Shake with ice and strain into collins glass. Sprinkle with nutmeg.

SCOTCH MIST

Pack old-fashioned glass with crushed ice. Pour in 2 oz. Desmond & Duff Scotch Whisky. *Add twist of lemon peel. Serve with short straw.*

SCOTCH OLD FASHIONED

Make same as Old Fashioned Cocktail (see page 105), but substitute Desmond & Duff Scotch Whisky.

SCOTCH RICKEY

Juice ½ Lime
1½ oz. Desmond & Duff
    Scotch Whisky
Pour into highball glass over ice and fill with carbonated water. Add rind of lime. Stir.

SCOTCH SOUR

1½ oz. Desmond & Duff
    Scotch Whisky
Juice ½ Lime
½ teaspoon Powdered Sugar
Shake with ice and strain into sour glass. Decorate with a half-slice of lemon and a cherry.

SCOTCH STINGER

Make same as Stinger Cocktail on page 142, but substitute Desmond & Duff Scotch Whisky *for brandy.*

SCOTCH WHISKY HIGHBALL

Put 2 oz. Desmond & Duff Scotch Whisky *in highball glass with ice cubes and fill with ginger ale or carbonated water. Add twist of lemon peel, if desired, and stir.*

SCREWDRIVER

Put two or three cubes of ice into highball glass. Add 2 oz. Old Mr. Boston Vodka. *Fill balance of glass with orange juice and stir.*

SEABOABD

1 oz. Old Thompson
    Blended Whiskey
1 oz. Old Mr. Boston Dry Gin
1 tablespoon Lemon Juice
1 teaspoon Powdered Sugar
Shake with ice and strain into old-fashioned glass over ice cubes. Decorate with mint leaves.

SENSATION COCKTAIL

Juice ¼ Lemon
1½ oz. Old Mr. Boston
    Dry Gin
1 teaspoon Maraschino
Shake with ice and strain into cocktail glass. Add two sprigs fresh mint.

SEPTEMBER MORN COCKTAIL

1 Egg White
1½ oz. Old Mr. Boston Rum
Juice ½ Lime
1 teaspoon Grenadine
Shake with ice and strain into cocktail glass.

SEVENTH HEAVEN COCKTAIL

2 teaspoons Grapefruit Juice
1 tablespoon Maraschino
1½ oz. Old Mr. Boston Dry Gin
Shake with ice and strain into cocktail glass. Decorate with sprig of fresh mint.

SEVILLA COCKTAIL

½ teaspoon Powdered Sugar
1 Whole Egg
1 oz. Port
1 oz. Old Mr. Boston Rum
Shake with ice and strain into flip glass.

SHADY GROVE

1½ oz. Old Mr. Boston Dry Gin
Juice ½ Lemon
1 teaspoon Powdered Sugar
Shake with ice and strain into highball glass with ice cubes. Fill with ginger beer.

SHALOM

1½ oz. Old Mr. Boston 100 Proof Vodka
1 oz. Madeira
1 tablespoon Orange Juice
Shake with ice and strain into old-fashioned glass over ice cubes. Add orange slice.

SHAMROCK COCKTAIL

1½ oz. Irish Whisky
½ oz. Dry Vermouth
1 teaspoon Old Mr. Boston Crème de Menthe (Green)
Stir with ice and strain into cocktail glass. Serve with an olive.

SHANDY GAFF

5 oz. Beer
5 oz. Ginger Ale
Pour into collins glass and stir.

SHANGHAI COCKTAIL

Juice ¼ Lemon
1 teaspoon Old Mr. Boston Anisette
1 oz. Jamaica Rum
½ teaspoon Grenadine
Shake with ice and strain into cocktail glass.

SHAVETAIL

1½ oz. Mr. Boston Peppermint Schnapps
1 oz. Pineapple Juice
1 oz. Sweet Cream
Shake with ice and strain into old-fashioned glass.

SHERRY-AND-EGG COCKTAIL

Place an egg in a cocktail glass, being careful not to break the yolk. Fill glass with sherry.

SHERRY COBBLER

In a goblet dissolve 1 teaspoon powdered sugar in 2 oz. carbonated water. Fill goblet with ice and add 2 oz. Sherry. Stir and decorate with fruits in season. Serve with straws.

SHERRY COCKTAIL

2½ oz. Sherry
1 dash Bitters
Stir with ice and strain into cocktail glass. Add a twist of orange peel.

SHERRY EGGNOG

1 Whole Egg
1 teaspoon Powdered Sugar
2 oz. Sherry
Shake above ingredients with ice and strain into collins glass. Fill glass with milk and stir. Sprinkle nutmeg on top.

SHERRY FLIP

1 Whole Egg
1 teaspoon Powdered Sugar
1½ oz. Sherry
2 teaspoons Sweet Cream
   (if desired)
Shake with ice and strain into flip glass. Sprinkle a little nutmeg on top.

SHERRY MILK PUNCH

1 teaspoon Powdered Sugar
2 oz. Sherry
½ pt. Milk
Shake with ice, strain into collins glass, and sprinkle nutmeg on top.

SHERRY SANGAREE

In an old-fashioned glass dissolve ½ teaspoon powdered sugar in 1 teaspoon water. Add 2 oz. Sherry and stir. Add ice cubes and a splash of carbonated water, leaving enough room on which to float a tablespoon of Port. Sprinkle lightly with nutmeg.

SHERRY TWIST COCKTAIL

1 oz. Sherry
½ oz. Old Mr. Boston
   Five Star Brandy
½ oz. Dry Vermouth
½ oz. Old Mr. Boston
   Triple Sec
½ teaspoon Lemon Juice
Shake with ice and strain into cocktail glass. Top with pinch of cinnamon and a twist of orange peel.

SHRINER COCKTAIL

1½ oz. Old Mr. Boston
   Five Star Brandy
1½ oz. Old Mr. Boston
   Sloe Gin
2 dashes Bitters
½ teaspoon Sugar Syrup
Stir with ice and strain into cocktail glass. Add a twist of lemon peel.

SIDECAR COCKTAIL

Juice ¼ Lemon
½ oz. Old Mr. Boston
   Triple Sec
1 oz. Old Mr. Boston
   Five Star Brandy
Shake with ice and strain into cocktail glass.

OLD Mr. BOSTON

SILVER BULLET

1 oz. Old Mr. Boston
    Dry Gin
1 oz. Kümmel
1 tablespoon Lemon Juice
Shake with ice and strain into cocktail glass.

SILVER COCKTAIL

1 oz. Dry Vermouth
1 oz. Old Mr. Boston Dry Gin
2 dashes Orange Bitters
¼ teaspoon Sugar Syrup
½ teaspoon Maraschino
Stir with ice and strain into cocktail glass. Add a twist of lemon peel.

SILVER FIZZ

Juice ½ Lemon
1 teaspoon Powdered Sugar
2 oz. Old Mr. Boston Dry Gin
1 Egg White
Shake with ice and strain into highball glass over two cubes of ice. Fill with carbonated water and stir.

SILVER KING COCKTAIL

1 Egg White
Juice ¼ Lemon
1½ oz. Old Mr. Boston
    Dry Gin
½ teaspoon Powdered Sugar
2 dashes Orange Bitters
Shake with ice and strain into cocktail glass.

SILVER STALLION FIZZ

1 scoop Vanilla Ice Cream
2 oz. Old Mr. Boston Dry Gin
Shake with ice and strain into highball glass. Fill with carbonated water and stir.

SILVER STREAK

1½ oz. Old Mr. Boston
    Dry Gin
1 oz. Kümmel
Shake with ice and strain into cocktail glass.

SINGAPORE SLING

Juice ½ Lemon
1 teaspoon Powdered Sugar
2 oz. Old Mr. Boston
    Dry Gin
Shake with ice and strain into collins glass. Add ice cubes and fill with carbonated water. Float on top ½ oz. Old Mr. Boston Wild Cherry Flavored Brandy. Decorate with fruits in season and serve with straws.

SIR WALTER COCKTAIL

¾ oz. Old Mr. Boston Rum
¾ oz. Old Mr. Boston
    Five Star Brandy
1 teaspoon Grenadine
1 teaspoon Old Mr. Boston
    Triple Sec
1 teaspoon Lemon Juice
Shake with ice and strain into cocktail glass.

SLINGS

See Index on page 208 for complete list of Sling recipes.

SLOE DRIVER

Put two or three cubes of ice into highball glass and add 2 oz. Old Mr. Boston Sloe Gin. Fill with orange juice and stir.

SLOE GIN COCKTAIL

2 oz. Old Mr. Boston
   Sloe Gin
1 dash Orange Bitters
¼ teaspoon Dry Vermouth
Stir with ice and strain into cocktail glass.

SLOE GIN COLLINS

Juice ½ Lemon
2 oz. Old Mr. Boston
   Sloe Gin
Shake with ice and strain into collins glass. Add several cubes of ice, fill with carbonated water and stir. Decorate with slices of lemon, orange, and a cherry. Serve with straws.

SLOE GIN FIZZ

Juice ½ Lemon
1 teaspoon Powdered Sugar
2 oz. Old Mr. Boston
   Sloe Gin
Shake with ice and strain into highball glass with two cubes of ice. Fill with carbonated water and stir. Decorate with slice of lemon.

SLOE GIN FLIP

1 Whole Egg
1 teaspoon Powdered Sugar
1 tablespoon Old Mr. Boston
   Sloe Gin
2 teaspoons Sweet Cream
   (if desired)
Shake with ice and strain into flip glass. Sprinkle a little nutmeg on top.

SLOE GIN RICKEY

Juice ½ Lime
2 oz. Old Mr. Boston
   Sloe Gin
Pour into highball glass over ice cubes and fill with carbonated water. Stir. Drop lime rind into glass.

SLOEBERRY COCKTAIL

1 dash Bitters
2 oz. Old Mr. Boston
   Sloe Gin
Stir with ice and strain into cocktail glass.

SLOE TEQUILA

1 oz. Gavilan Tequila
½ oz. Old Mr. Boston
   Sloe Gin
1 tablespoon Lime Juice
Combine ingredients with half a cup of crushed ice in a blender. Blend at low speed and pour into old-fashioned glass. Add ice cubes and cucumber peel.

SLOE VERMOUTH

1 oz. Old Mr. Boston
  Sloe Gin
1 oz. Dry Vermouth
1 tablespoon Lemon Juice
Shake with ice and strain into cocktail glass.

SLOPPY JOE'S COCKTAIL No. 1

Juice 1 Lime
¼ teaspoon Old Mr. Boston
  Triple Sec
¼ teaspoon Grenadine
¾ oz. Old Mr. Boston Rum
¾ oz. Dry Vermouth
Shake with ice and strain into cocktail glass.

SLOPPY JOE'S COCKTAIL No. 2

¾ oz. Pineapple Juice
¾ oz. Old Mr. Boston
  Five Star Brandy
¾ oz. Port
¼ teaspoon Old Mr. Boston
  Triple Sec
¼ teaspoon Grenadine
Shake with ice and strain into cocktail glass.

SMASHES

See Index on page 209 for complete list of Smash recipes.

SMILE COCKTAIL

1 oz. Grenadine
1 oz. Old Mr. Boston Dry Gin
½ teaspoon Lemon Juice
Shake with ice and strain into cocktail glass.

SMILER COCKTAIL

½ oz. Sweet Vermouth
½ oz. Dry Vermouth
1 oz. Old Mr. Boston Dry Gin
1 dash Bitters
¼ teaspoon Orange Juice
Shake with ice and strain into cocktail glass.

SNOWBALL COCKTAIL

1½ oz. Old Mr. Boston
  Dry Gin
½ oz. Old Mr. Boston
  Anisette
1 tablespoon Sweet Cream
Shake with ice and strain into cocktail glass.

SNYDER

1½ oz. Old Mr. Boston
  Dry Gin
½ oz. Dry Vermouth
½ oz. Old Mr. Boston
  Triple Sec
Shake with ice and strain into cocktail glass. Add a twist of lemon peel.

SOCIETY COCKTAIL

1½ oz. Old Mr. Boston
  Dry Gin
¾ oz. Dry Vermouth
¼ teaspoon Grenadine
Stir with ice and strain into cocktail glass.

SOMBRERO

1½ oz. Old Mr. Boston
  Coffee Flavored Brandy
1 oz. Sweet Cream
Pour brandy into old-fashioned glass over ice cubes. Float cream on top.

SOOTHER COCKTAIL

½ oz. Old Mr. Boston
    Five Star Brandy
½ oz. Apple Brandy
½ oz. Old Mr. Boston
    Triple Sec
Juice ½ Lemon
1 teaspoon Powdered Sugar
*Shake with ice and strain into
cocktail glass.*

SOUL KISS COCKTAIL

1½ teaspoons Orange Juice
1½ teaspoons Dubonnet
¾ oz. Dry Vermouth
¾ oz. Old Kentucky Tavern
    Bourbon Whiskey
*Shake with ice and strain into
cocktail glass.*

SOURS

*See Index on page 209 for
complete list of Sour recipes.*

SOUTHERN BRIDE

1½ oz. Old Mr. Boston
    Dry Gin
1 oz. Grapefruit Juice
1 dash Maraschino
*Shake with ice and strain into
cocktail glass.*

SOUTHERN GIN COCKTAIL

2 oz. Old Mr. Boston Dry Gin
2 dashes Orange Bitters
½ teaspoon Old Mr. Boston
    Triple Sec
*Stir with ice and strain into
cocktail glass. Add a twist of
lemon peel.*

SOUTH OF THE BORDER

1 oz. Gavilan Tequila
¾ oz. Old Mr. Boston
    Coffee Flavored Brandy
Juice ½ Lime
*Shake with ice and strain into
sour glass. Add lime slice.*

SOUTH-SIDE COCKTAIL

Juice ½ Lemon
1 teaspoon Powdered Sugar
1½ oz. Old Mr. Boston
    Dry Gin
*Shake with ice and strain into
cocktail glass. Add two sprigs
of fresh mint.*

SOUTH-SIDE FIZZ

Juice ½ Lemon
1 teaspoon Powdered Sugar
2 oz. Old Mr. Boston Dry Gin
*Shake with ice and strain into
highball glass with ice cubes.
Fill with carbonated water
and stir. Add fresh mint
leaves.*

SOVIET

1½ oz. Old Mr. Boston
    Vodka
½ oz. Amontillado
    Sherry
½ oz. Dry Vermouth
Shake with ice and strain into old-fashioned glass over ice cubes. Add a twist of lemon peel.

SPANISH TOWN COCKTAIL

2 oz. Old Mr. Boston Rum
1 teaspoon Old Mr. Boston
    Triple Sec
Stir with ice and strain into cocktail glass.

SPECIAL ROUGH COCKTAIL

1½ oz. Apple Brandy
1½ oz. Old Mr. Boston
    Five Star Brandy
½ teaspoon Absinthe
    Substitute
Stir with ice and strain into cocktail glass.

SPENCER COCKTAIL

¾ oz. Old Mr. Boston
    Apricot Flavored Brandy
1½ oz. Old Mr. Boston
    Dry Gin
1 dash Bitters
¼ teaspoon Orange Juice
Shake with ice and strain into cocktail glass. Add a cherry and twist of orange peel.

SPHINX COCKTAIL

1½ oz. Old Mr. Boston
    Dry Gin
1½ teaspoons Sweet
    Vermouth
1½ teaspoon Dry Vermouth
Stir with ice and strain into cocktail glass. Serve with slice of lemon.

SPRING FEELING COCKTAIL

1 tablespoon Lemon Juice
½ oz. Chartreuse (Green)
1 oz. Old Mr. Boston Dry Gin
Shake with ice and strain into cocktail glass.

SPRITZER HIGHBALL

Pour 3 oz. chilled Rhine wine or Sauterne into highball glass with ice cubes. Fill balance with carbonated water and stir gently.

STANLEY COCKTAIL

Juice ¼ Lemon
1 teaspoon Grenadine
¾ oz. Old Mr. Boston
    Dry Gin
¼ oz. Old Mr. Boston Rum
Shake with ice and strain into cocktail glass.

OLD Mr. BOSTON

STAR COCKTAIL

1 oz. Apple Brandy
1 oz. Sweet Vermouth
1 dash Bitters
Stir with ice and strain into cocktail glass. Add a twist of lemon peel.

STAR DAISY

Juice ½ Lemon
½ teaspoon Powdered Sugar
1 teaspoon Raspberry Syrup or Grenadine
1 oz. Old Mr. Boston Dry Gin
1 oz. Apple Brandy
Shake with ice and strain into stein or metal cup. Add cube of ice and decorate with fruit.

STARS AND STRIPES

⅓ Grenadine
⅓ Heavy Sweet Cream
⅓ Blue Curacao
Pour carefully, in order given, into pousse-café glass, so that each ingredient floats on preceding one.

STILETTO

Juice ½ Lemon
1½ teaspoons Amaretto Di Saronno
1½ oz. Old Kentucky Tavern Bourbon or Old Thompson Blended Whiskey
Pour into an old-fashioned glass over ice cubes and stir.

STINGER COCKTAIL

½ oz. Old Mr. Boston Crème de Menthe (White)
1½ oz. Old Mr. Boston Five Star Brandy
Shake with ice and strain into cocktail glass.

STIRRUP CUP

1 oz. Old Mr. Boston Wild Cherry Flavored Brandy
1 oz. Old Mr. Boston Five Star Brandy
Juice ½ Lemon
1 teaspoon Sugar
Shake with ice and strain into old-fashioned glass over ice cubes.

STONE COCKTAIL

½ oz. Old Mr. Boston Rum
½ oz. Sweet Vermouth
1 oz. Dry Sherry
Stir with ice and strain into cocktail glass.

STONE FENCE

2 dashes Bitters
2 oz. Desmond & Duff Scotch Whisky
Fill highball glass with ice cubes. Add scotch and bitters and fill with carbonated water or cider. Stir.

STRAIGHT LAW COCKTAIL

¾ oz. Old Mr. Boston Dry Gin
1½ oz. Dry Sherry
Stir with ice and strain into cocktail glass.

STRAWBERRY DAIQUIRI

1 oz. Mr. Boston Rum
½ oz. Strawberry Liqueur
1 oz. Lime Juice
1 teaspoon Powdered Sugar
1 oz. Fresh or Frozen
    Strawberries
Shake with ice and strain into cocktail glass.

STRAWBERRY MARGARITA

1 oz. Gavilan Tequila
½ oz. Mr. Boston Triple Sec
½ oz. Strawberry Liqueur
1 oz. Lemon or Lime Juice
1 oz. Fresh or Frozen
    Strawberries
If desired, rub rim of cocktail glass with rind of lemon or lime, dip rim in salt. Shake ingredients with ice and strain into the glass.

SUISSESSE COCKTAIL

2   oz. Old Mr. Boston
    Anisette
1 Egg White
Shake with ice and strain into cocktail glass.

SUNSHINE COCKTAIL

¾ oz. Sweet Vermouth
1½ oz. Old Mr. Boston
    Dry Gin
1 dash Bitters
Stir with ice and strain into cocktail glass. Add a twist of orange peel.

SUSIE TAYLOR

Juice ½ Lime
2 oz. Old Mr. Boston Rum
Pour into collins glass over ice cubes and fill with ginger ale. Stir.

SWEET MARIA

1 tablespoon Sweet Cream
½ oz. Amaretto Di Saronno
1 oz. Old Mr. Boston Vodka
Shake with cracked ice. Strain into cocktail glass.

SWEET PATOOTIE COCKTAIL

1 oz. Old Mr. Boston Dry Gin
½ oz. Old Mr. Boston
    Triple Sec
1 tablespoon Orange Juice
Shake with ice and strain into cocktail glass.

SWISS FAMILY COCKTAIL

½ teaspoon Absinthe
    Substitute
2 dashes Bitters
¾ oz. Dry Vermouth
1½ oz. Old Thompson
    Blended Whiskey
Stir with ice and strain into cocktail glass.

SWIZZLES

See Index on page 209 for complete list of Swizzle recipes.

TAHITI CLUB

2 oz. Old Mr. Boston Rum
1 tablespoon Lemon Juice
1 tablespoon Lime Juice
1 tablespoon Pineapple Juice
½ teaspoon Maraschino
Shake with ice and strain into old-fashioned glass over ice cubes. Add slice of lemon.

TAILSPIN COCKTAIL

¾ oz. Old Mr. Boston Dry Gin
¾ oz. Sweet Vermouth
¾ oz. Chartreuse (Green)
1 dash Orange Bitters
Stir with ice and strain into cocktail glass. Add a twist of lemon peel and a cherry or olive.

TANGO COCKTAIL

1 tablespoon Orange Juice
½ oz. Dry Vermouth
½ oz. Sweet Vermouth
1 oz. Old Mr. Boston Dry Gin
½ teaspoon Old Mr. Boston Triple Sec
Shake with ice and strain into cocktail glass.

TCHOUPITOLAS STREET GUZZLE

1 oz. Old Mr. Boston Rum
1 Split Ginger Beer
Pour rum into highball glass over ice cubes. Add ginger beer.

TEA SARONNO

6 oz. freshly brewed hot tea
1½ to 2 oz. Amaretto di Saronno
Whipped Cream
Pour hot tea into a stemmed glass, using a spoon in glass to prevent cracking. Add Amaretto di Saronno *but do not stir. Top with chilled whipped cream.*

TEMPTATION COCKTAIL

1½ oz. Old Thompson Blended Whiskey
½ teaspoon Old Mr. Boston Triple Sec
½ teaspoon Absinthe Substitute
½ teaspoon Dubonnet
Shake with ice and strain into cocktail glass. Add twists of lemon and orange peel.

TEMPTER COCKTAIL

1 oz. Port
1 oz. Old Mr. Boston Apricot Flavored Brandy
Stir with ice and strain into cocktail glass.

TEQUILA COLLINS

Make same as Tom Collins (see page 150) but use Gavilan Tequila *instead of dry gin.*

TEQUILA FIZZ

2 oz. Gavilan Tequila
¾ oz. Grenadine
1 tablespoon Lemon Juice
1 Egg White
Shake well with ice and strain into collins glass over ice cubes. Fill with ginger ale and stir.

TEQUILA MANHATTAN

2 oz. Gavilan Tequila
1 oz. Sweet Vermouth
1 dash Lime Juice
Shake with ice and strain over ice cubes in old-fashioned glass. Add a cherry and an orange slice.

TEQUILA MATADOR

1½ oz. Gavilan Tequila
3 oz. Pineapple Juice
Juice ½ Lime
Shake with crushed ice and strain into champagne glass.

TEQUILA MOCKINGBIRD

1½ oz. Gavilan Tequila
¾ oz. Old Mr. Boston
  Creme de Menthe (Green)
Juice 1 Lime
Shake with ice and strain into cocktail glass. Decorate with lime slice.

TEQUILA OLD FASHIONED

1½ oz. Gavilan Tequila
½ teaspoon Sugar
1 dash Bitters
Mix sugar, bitters, and a teaspoon of water in old-fash-ioned glass. Add tequila, ice, and a splash of carbonated water. Decorate with pine-apple stick.

TEQUILA PINK

1½ oz. Gavilan Tequila
1 oz. Dry Vermouth
1 dash Grenadine
Shake with ice and strain into cocktail glass.

TEQUILA PUNCH

1 qt. Gavilan Tequila
1 bottle Champagne
4 bottles Sauterne
2 qts. Fresh Fruits (Cubes
  or Balls)
Sweeten to taste, chill thor-oughly, and add ice cubes just before serving. Place in large bowl and serve in sherbet cups.

TEQUILA SOUR

Juice ½ Lemon
1 teaspoon Powdered Sugar
2 oz. Gavilan Tequila
Shake with ice and strain into sour glass. Decorate with half a slice of lemon and a cherry.

TEQUILA STRAIGHT

¼ Lemon
1 pinch Salt
1½ oz. Gavilan Tequila
Put salt between thumb and index finger on back of left hand. Hold jigger of Tequila in same hand and the lemon wedge in right hand. Taste salt, drink the tequila, and then suck the lemon.

TEQUILA SUNRISE

2 oz. Gavilan Tequila
4 oz. Orange Juice
¾ oz. Grenadine

*Stir tequila and orange juice
with ice and strain into highball glass. Add ice cubes. Pour
in grenadine slowly and allow
to settle. Before drinking, stir
to complete your Sunrise.*

TEQUINI COCKTAIL

1½ oz. Gavilan Tequila
½ oz. Dry Vermouth
1 dash Bitters (if desired)

*Stir with ice and strain into
cocktail glass. Serve with twist
of lemon peel and an olive.*

TEQUONIC

2 oz. Gavilan Tequila
Juice ½ Lemon or Lime

*Pour tequila over ice cubes in
old-fashioned glass. Add fruit
juice, fill with tonic water and
stir.*

THANKSGIVING SPECIAL COCKTAIL

¾ oz. Old Mr. Boston
    Apricot Flavored Brandy
¾ oz. Old Mr. Boston
    Dry Gin
¾ oz. Dry Vermouth
¼ teaspoon Lemon Juice

*Shake with ice and strain into
cocktail glass. Serve with a
cherry.*

THE SHOOT

1 oz. Desmond & Duff
    Scotch Whisky
1 oz. Dry Sherry
1 teaspoon Orange Juice
1 teaspoon Lemon Juice
½ teaspoon Powdered Sugar

*Shake with ice and strain into
cocktail glass.*

THIRD DEGREE COCKTAIL

1½ oz. Old Mr. Boston
    Dry Gin
¾ oz. Dry Vermouth
1 teaspoon Absinthe
    Substitute

*Stir with ice and strain into
cocktail glass.*

THIRD RAIL COCKTAIL

¾ oz. Old Mr. Boston Rum
¾ oz. Apple Brandy
¾ oz. Old Mr. Boston
    Five Star Brandy
¼ teaspoon Absinthe
    Substitute

*Shake with ice and strain into
cocktail glass.*

THISTLE COCKTAIL

1½ oz. Sweet Vermouth
1½ oz. Desmond & Duff
    Scotch Whisky
2 dashes Bitters

*Stir with ice and strain into
cocktail glass.*

THREE MILLER COCKTAIL

1½ oz. Old Mr. Boston Rum
¾ oz. Old Mr. Boston
    Five Star Brandy
1 teaspoon Grenadine
¼ teaspoon Lemon Juice

*Shake with ice and strain into
cocktail glass.*

OLD Mr. BOSTON

THREE STRIPES COCKTAIL
1 oz. Old Mr. Boston Dry Gin
½ oz. Dry Vermouth
1 tablespoon Orange Juice
Shake with ice and strain into cocktail glass.

THUNDER COCKTAIL
1 teaspoon Powered Sugar
1 Egg Yolk
1½ oz. Old Mr. Boston
    Five Star Brandy
1 pinch Cayenne Pepper
Shake with ice and strain into cocktail glass.

THUNDER-AND-LIGHTNING COCKTAIL
1 Egg Yolk
1 teaspoon Powdered Sugar
1½ oz. Old Mr. Boston
    Five Star Brandy
Shake with ice and strain into cocktail glass.

THUNDERCLAP COCKTAIL
¾ oz. Old Mr. Boston
    Dry Gin
¾ oz. Old Thompson
    Blended Whiskey
¾ oz. Old Mr. Boston
    Five Star Brandy
Shake with ice and strain into cocktail glass.

TIDBIT
1 oz. Old Mr. Boston Dry Gin
1 scoop Vanilla Ice Cream
1 dash Dry Sherry
Blend at low speed and pour into highball glass.

TIPPERARY COCKTAIL
¾ oz. Irish Whisky
¾ oz. Chartreuse (Green)
¾ oz. Sweet Vermouth
Stir well with ice and strain into cocktail glass.

T.N.T. COCKTAIL
1½ oz. Old Thompson
    Blended Whiskey
1½ oz. Absinthe Substitute
Shake with ice and strain into cocktail glass.

TODDIES
See Index on page 210 for complete list of Toddy recipes.

TOM-AND-JERRY
First prepare batter, using mixing bowl. Separate the yolk and white of one egg, beating each separately and thoroughly. Then combine both, adding enough superfine powdered sugar to stiffen. Add to this one pinch of baking soda and ¼ oz. Old Mr. Boston Rum to preserve the batter. Then add a little more sugar to stiffen. To serve, use hot Tom-and-Jerry mug, using one tablespoon of above batter, dissolved in 3 tablespoons hot milk. Add 1½ oz. Old

Amaretto di Saronno—a liqueur—56 Proof ▶

Mr. Boston Rum. *Then fill mug with hot milk within ¼ inch of the top of the mug and stir. Then top with ½ oz. Old Mr. Boston Brandy and sprinkle a little nutmeg on top. The secret of a Tom-and-Jerry is to have a stiff batter and a warm mug.*

TOMBOY

½ cup Chilled Tomato Juice
½ cup Cold Beer
Pour tomato juice into highball glass. Add beer.

TOM COLLINS

Juice ½ Lemon
1 teaspoon Powdered Sugar
2 oz. Old Mr. Boston Dry Gin
Shake with ice and strain into collins glass. Add several cubes of ice, fill with carbonated water, and stir. Decorate with slices of lemon, orange and a cherry. Serve with straw.

TOP BANANA

1 oz. Old Mr. Boston Vodka
1 oz. Old Mr. Boston
　　Crème de Banana
Juice ½ Orange
Shake with ice and strain into old-fashioned glass over ice cubes.

TOREADOR

1½ oz. Gavilan Tequila
½ oz. Old Mr. Boston
　　Creme de Cacao
1 tablespoon Sweet Cream
Shake with ice and strain into cocktail glass. Top with a little whipped cream and sprinkle lightly with cocoa.

TORRIDORA COCKTAIL

1½ oz. Old Mr. Boston Rum
½ oz. Old Mr. Boston
　　Coffee Flavored Brandy
1½ teaspoons Sweet Cream
Shake with ice, strain into cocktail glass. Float 1 teaspoon of 151 Proof Rum on top.

TOVARICH COCKTAIL

1½ oz. Old Mr. Boston
　　Vodka
¾ oz. Kümmel
Juice ½ Lime
Shake with ice and strain into cocktail glass.

TRILBY COCKTAIL

1½ oz. Old Kentucky Tavern
　　Bourbon Whiskey
¾ oz. Sweet Vermouth
2 dashes Orange Bitters
Stir with ice and strain into cocktail glass.

TRINITY COCKTAIL

¾ oz. Sweet Vermouth
¾ oz. Dry Vermouth
¾ oz. Old Mr. Boston
　　Dry Gin
Stir with ice and strain into cocktail glass.

TROIS RIVIÈRES

1½ oz. Old Mr. Boston Five
    Star Canadian Whisky
1 tablespoon Dubonnet
1½ teaspoons Old Mr. Boston
    Triple Sec

Shake with ice and strain into old-fashioned glass over ice cubes. Add twist of orange peel.

TROPICAL COCKTAIL

¾ oz. Old Mr. Boston
    Crème de Cacao (White)
¾ oz. Maraschino
¾ oz. Dry Vermouth
1 dash Bitters

Stir with ice and strain into cocktail glass.

TULIP COCKTAIL

1½ teaspoons Lemon Juice
1½ teaspoons Old Mr. Boston
    Apricot Flavored Brandy
¾ oz. Sweet Vermouth
¾ oz. Apple Brandy

Shake with ice and strain into cocktail glass.

TURF COCKTAIL

¼ teaspoon Absinthe
    Substitute
2 dashes Bitters
1 oz. Dry Vermouth
1 oz. Old Mr. Boston Dry Gin

Stir with ice and strain into cocktail glass. Add a twist of orange peel.

TUXEDO COCKTAIL

1½ oz. Old Mr. Boston
    Dry Gin
1½ oz. Dry Vermouth
¼ teaspoon Maraschino
¼ teaspoon Absinthe
    Substitute
2 dashes Orange Bitters

Stir with ice and strain into cocktail glass. Serve with a cherry.

TWIN HILLS

1½ oz. Old Thompson
    Blended Whiskey
2 teaspoons Benedictine
1½ teaspoons Lemon Juice
1½ teaspoons Lime Juice
1 teaspoon Sugar

Shake with ice and strain into sour glass. Add slice of lime and of lemon.

OLD MR. BOSTON

TWIN SIX COCKTAIL

1 oz. Old Mr. Boston Dry Gin
½ oz. Sweet Vermouth
¼ teaspoon Grenadine
1 tablespoon Orange Juice
1 Egg White
Shake with ice and strain into cocktail glass.

TWISTER

2 oz. Old Mr. Boston Vodka
Juice ⅓ Lime
Pour into collins glass. Add several cubes of ice, drop lime rind into glass. Fill with lemon soda and stir.

TYPHOON

1 oz. Old Mr. Boston Dry Gin
½ oz. Old Mr. Boston Anisette
1 oz. Lime Juice
Shake all ingredients with ice. Strain into collins glass with ice cubes. Fill glass with chilled champagne.

U

ULANDA COCKTAIL
1½ oz. Old Mr. Boston
   Dry Gin
¾ oz. Old Mr. Boston
   Triple Sec
¼ teaspoon Absinthe
   Substitute
Stir with ice and strain into cocktail glass.

UNION JACK COCKTAIL
¾ oz. Mr. Boston Sloe Gin
1½ oz. Old Mr. Boston
   Dry Gin
½ teaspoon Grenadine
Shake with ice and strain into cocktail glass.

VALENCIA COCKTAIL

1 tablespoon Orange Juice
1½ oz. Old Mr. Boston
    Apricot Flavored Brandy
2 dashes Orange Bitters
Shake with ice and strain into cocktail glass.

VANDERBILT COCKTAIL

¾ oz. Old Mr. Boston Wild
    Cherry Flavored Brandy
1½ oz. Old Mr. Boston
    Five Star Brandy
1 teaspoon Sugar Syrup
2 dashes Bitters
Stir with ice and strain into cocktail glass.

VAN VLEET

3 oz. Old Mr. Boston Rum
1 oz. Maple Syrup
1 oz. Lemon Juice
Shake well with ice and strain into old-fashioned glass over ice cubes.

VELVET HAMMER NO. 1

1½ oz. Old Mr. Boston
    Vodka
1 tablespoon Old Mr. Boston
    Crème de Cacao
1 tablespoon Sweet Cream
Shake with ice and strain into cocktail glass.

VELVET HAMMER NO. 2

1½ oz. Strega
1 oz. Old Mr. Boston
    Crème de Cacao (White)
1 tablespoon Sweet Cream
Shake with ice and strain into cocktail glass.

VERBOTEN

1½ oz. Old Mr. Boston
    Dry Gin
1 tablespoon Forbidden Fruit
1 tablespoon Orange Juice
1 tablespoon Lemon Juice
Shake with ice and strain into cocktail glass. Add brandied cherry.

VERMOUTH CASSIS

¾ oz. Mr. Boston
    Crème de Cassis
1½ oz. Dry Vermouth
Stir in highball glass with ice cubes and fill with carbonated water. Stir again and serve.

OLD Mr. BOSTON

VERMOUTH COCKTAIL

1 oz. Dry Vermouth
1 oz. Sweet Vermouth
1 dash Orange Bitters
Stir with ice and strain into cocktail glass. Serve with a cherry.

VESUVIO

1 oz. Old Mr. Boston Rum
Juice ½ Lemon
1 teaspoon Powdered Sugar
½ Egg White
½ oz. Sweet Vermouth
Shake with ice and strain into old-fashioned glass over ice cubes.

VICTOR

1½ oz. Old Mr. Boston
    Dry Gin
½ oz. Old Mr. Boston
    Five Star Brandy
½ oz. Sweet Vermouth
Shake with ice and strain into cocktail glass.

VICTORY COLLINS

1½ oz. Old Mr. Boston
    Vodka
3 oz. Unsweetened Grape
    Juice
3 oz. Lemon Juice
1 teaspoon Powdered Sugar
Shake with ice and strain into collins glass with ice cubes. Add slice of orange.

VIRGIN

1 oz. Old Mr. Boston Dry Gin
½ oz. Old Mr. Boston
    Crème de Menthe (White)
1 oz. Forbidden Fruit
Shake with ice and strain into cocktail glass.

VIVA VILLA

Juice 1 Lime
1 teaspoon Sugar
1½ oz. Gavilan Tequila
Shake with ice and strain over ice cubes into old-fashioned glass, rimmed with salt.

VODKA-AND-APPLE JUICE

Put two or three cubes of ice into highball glass. Add 2 oz. Old Mr. Boston Vodka. Fill balance of glass with apple juice and stir.

VODKA AND TONIC

Pour 2 oz. Old Mr. Boston Vodka into highball glass over ice cubes, add quinine water, and stir.

VODKA COLLINS

Make same as Tom Collins (see page 150) but use Old Mr. Boston Vodka instead of Gin.

OLD Mr. BOSTON

VODKA COOLER

Make same as **Gin Cooler** (see page 63) but use Old Mr. Boston Vodka instead of gin.

VODKA DAISY

Juice ½ Lemon
½ teaspoon Powdered Sugar
1 teaspoon Grenadine
2 oz. Old Mr. Boston Vodka
Shake with ice and strain into stein or metal cup. Add ice cubes and decorate with fruit.

VODKA GIMLET COCKTAIL

Make same as Gimlet Cocktail (see page 62) but use Old Mr. Boston Vodka instead of gin.

VODKA GRASSHOPPER COCKTAIL

¾ oz. Old Mr. Boston Vodka
¾ oz. Old Mr. Boston
    Crème de Menthe (Green)
¾ oz. Old Mr. Boston
    Crème de Cacao (White)
Shake with ice and strain into cocktail glass.

VODKA GYPSY COCKTAIL

1½ oz. Old Mr. Boston
    Vodka
¾ oz. Benedictine
1 dash Angostura Bitters
Stir with ice and strain into cocktail glass.

VODKA MARTINI COCKTAIL

See Special Martini Section on pages 173 and 174

VODKA-ON-THE-ROCKS

Put two or three cubes of ice in old-fashioned glass and add 2 oz. Old Mr. Boston Vodka. Serve with a twist of lemon peel.

VODKA SALTY DOG

1½ oz. Old Mr. Boston Vodka
5 oz. Grapefruit Juice
¼ teaspoon Salt
Pour into highball glass over ice cubes. Stir well.

VODKA "7"

2 oz. Old Mr. Boston Vodka
Juice ½ Lime
Pour into collins glass over cubes of ice. Drop lime rind in glass, fill balance with lemon soda and stir.

VODKA SLING

Make same as Gin Sling (see page 64) but use Old Mr. Boston Vodka instead of gin.

VODKA SOUR

Juice ½ Lemon
½ teaspoon Powdered Sugar
2 oz. Old Mr. Boston Vodka
Shake with ice and strain into sour glass. Decorate with half-slice of lemon and a cherry.

VODKA STINGER

1 oz. Old Mr. Boston Vodka
1 oz. Old Mr. Boston
    Crème de Menthe (White)
Shake with ice and strain into cocktail glass.

W

WAIKIKI BEACHCOMBER

¾ oz. Old Mr. Boston
    Dry Gin
¾ oz. Old Mr. Boston
    Triple Sec
1 tablespoon Fresh Pineapple
    Juice
Shake with ice and strain into cocktail glass.

WALLICK COCKTAIL

1½ oz. Dry Vermouth
1½ oz. Old Mr. Boston
    Dry Gin
1 teaspoon Old Mr. Boston
    Triple Sec
Stir with ice and strain into cocktail glass.

WALLIS BLUE COCKTAIL

1 oz. Old Mr. Boston
    Triple Sec
1 oz. Old Mr. Boston Dry Gin
Juice 1 Lime
Moisten rim of an old-fashioned glass with lime juice and dip into powdered sugar. Shake ingredients with ice and strain into prepared glass over ice cubes.

WALTERS

1½ oz. Desmond & Duff
    Scotch Whisky
1 tablespoon Orange Juice
1 tablespoon Lemon Juice
Shake with ice and strain into cocktail glass.

WARD EIGHT

Juice ½ Lemon
1 teaspoon Powdered Sugar
1 teaspoon Grenadine
2 oz. Old Thompson
    Blended Whiskey
Shake with ice and strain into goblet filled with cracked ice. Add slices of orange, lemon and a cherry. Serve with straws.

WARSAW COCKTAIL

1½ oz. Old Mr. Boston
    Vodka
½ oz. Old Mr. Boston
    Blackberry Flavored
    Brandy
½ oz. Dry Vermouth
1 teaspoon Lemon Juice
Shake with ice and strain into cocktail glass.

WASHINGTON COCKTAIL

1½ oz. Dry Vermouth
¾ oz. Old Mr. Boston
    Five Star Brandy
2 dashes Bitters
½ teaspoon Sugar Syrup
Stir with ice and strain into cocktail glass.

OLD Mr. BOSTON

WATERBURY COCKTAIL
½ teaspoon Powdered Sugar
Juice ¼ Lemon or ½ Lime
1 Egg White
1½ oz. Old Mr. Boston
    Five Star Brandy
½ teaspoon Grenadine
Shake with ice and strain into cocktail glass.

WEBSTER COCKTAIL
Juice ½ Lime
1½ teaspoons Old Mr. Boston
    Apricot Flavored Brandy
½ oz. Dry Vermouth
1 oz. Old Mr. Boston Dry Gin
Shake with ice and strain into cocktail glass.

WEDDING BELLE COCKTAIL
1½ teaspoons Orange Juice
1½ teaspoons Old Mr. Boston
    Wild Cherry Flavored
    Brandy
¾ oz. Old Mr. Boston
    Dry Gin
¾ oz. Dubonnet
Shake with ice and strain into cocktail glass.

WEEP-NO-MORE COCKTAIL
Juice ½ Lime
¾ oz. Dubonnet
¾ oz. Old Mr. Boston
    Five Star Brandy
¼ teaspoon Maraschino
Shake with ice and strain into cocktail glass.

WEMBLY COCKTAIL
¾ oz. Dry Vermouth
1½ oz. Old Mr. Boston
    Dry Gin
¼ teaspoon Old Mr. Boston
    Apricot Flavored Brandy
½ teaspoon Apple Brandy
Stir with ice and strain into cocktail glass.

WEST INDIAN PUNCH
2 Qts. Old Mr. Boston Rum
1 Fifth Old Mr. Boston
    Crème de Banana
1 Qt. Pineapple Juice
1 Qt. Orange Juice
1 Qt. Lemon Juice
¾ Cup Powdered Sugar
1 teaspoon Grated Nutmeg
1 teaspoon Cinnamon
½ teaspoon Grated Cloves
Dissolve sugar and spices in 6 oz. carbonated water. Pour into large punchbowl over block of ice, and add other ingredients. Stir and decorate with sliced bananas.

WESTERN ROSE COCKTAIL
½ oz. Old Mr. Boston
    Apricot Flavored Brandy
1 oz. Old Mr. Boston Dry Gin
½ oz. Dry Vermouth
¼ teaspoon Lemon Juice
Shake with ice and strain into cocktail glass.

WHISKEY COCKTAIL

1 dash Angostura bitters
1 teaspoon Sugar Syrup
2 oz. Old Thompson
    Blended Whiskey
Stir with ice and strain into cocktail glass. Serve with a cherry.

WHISKEY COLLINS

Juice ½ Lemon
1 teaspoon Powdered Sugar
2 oz. Old Thompson
    Blended Whiskey
Shake with ice and strain into collins glass. Add several cubes of ice, fill with carbonated water and stir. Decorate with slices of lemon, orange and a cherry. Serve with straw.

WHAT THE HELL

1 oz. Old Mr. Boston Dry Gin
1 oz. Dry Vermouth
1 oz. Old Mr. Boston
    Apricot Flavored Brandy
1 dash Lemon Juice
Stir in old-fashioned glass over ice cubes.

WHIP COCKTAIL

½ oz. Dry Vermouth
½ oz. Sweet Vermouth
1½ oz. Old Mr. Boston
    Five Star Brandy
¼ teaspoon Absinthe
    Substitute
1 teaspoon Old Mr. Boston
    Triple Sec
Stir with ice and strain into cocktail glass.

WHISKEY DAISY

Juice ½ Lemon
½ teaspoon Powdered Sugar
1 teaspoon Raspberry Syrup
    or Grenadine
2 oz. Old Thompson
    Blended Whiskey
Shake with ice and strain into stein or metal cup. Add cube of ice and decorate with fruit.

WHISKEY COBBLER

Dissolve one teaspoon powdered sugar in 2 oz. carbonated water in a goblet. Fill with shaved ice and add 2 oz. Old Thompson Blended Whiskey. Stir and decorate with fruits in season. Serve with straw.

WHISKEY EGGNOG

1 Whole Egg
1 teaspoon Powdered Sugar
2 oz. Old Thompson
    Blended Whiskey
Shake ingredients with ice and strain into collins glass. Fill glass with milk. Sprinkle nutmeg on top.

WHISKEY FIX

Juice ½ Lemon
1 teaspoon Powdered Sugar
Shake with ice and strain into highball glass. Fill glass with ice. Add 2½ oz. Old Thompson Blended Whiskey. Stir and add slice of lemon. Serve with straws.

WHISKEY FLIP

1 Whole Egg
1 teaspoon Powdered Sugar
1½ oz. Old Thompson
    Blended Whiskey
2 teaspoons Sweet Cream
    (if desired)
Shake with ice and strain into flip glass. Sprinkle a little nutmeg on top.

WHISKEY HIGHBALL

Pour 2 oz. Old Thompson Blended Whiskey *into highball glass over ice cubes and fill with ginger ale or carbonated water. Add twist of lemon peel, if desired, and stir.*

WHISKEY MILK PUNCH

1 teaspoon Powdered Sugar
2 oz. Old Thompson
    Blended Whiskey
½ pt. Milk
Shake with ice, strain into collins glass and sprinkle nutmeg on top.

WHISKEY ORANGE

Juice ½ Orange
1 teaspoon Powdered Sugar
½ teaspoon Absinthe
    Substitute
1½ oz. Old Thompson
    Blended Whiskey
Shake with ice and strain into highball glass over ice cubes. Decorate with slices of orange and lemon.

WHISKEY RICKEY

Juice ½ Lime
1½ oz. Old Thompson
    Blended Whiskey
Pour into highball glass over ice cubes and fill with carbonated water. Stir. Drop the lime rind into glass.

WHISKEY SANGAREE

In an old-fashioned glass, dissolve ½ teaspoon powdered sugar in 1 teaspoon of water and add 2 oz. Old Thompson Blended Whiskey. Add ice cubes and a splash of carbonated water. Stir and float a tablespoon of port on top. Sprinkle lightly with nutmeg.

WHISKEY SKIN

Put lump of sugar into hot whiskey glass and fill two-thirds with boiling water. Add 2 oz. Old Thompson Blended Whiskey. Stir, then add twist of lemon peel.

WHISKEY SLING

In an old-fashioned glass, dissolve one teaspoon powdered sugar in teaspoon of water and juice ½ lemon; add ice cubes and 2 oz. Old Thompson Blended Whiskey. Stir and add a twist of lemon peel.

WHISKEY SMASH

Muddle one lump of sugar in an old-fashioned glass with 1 oz. carbonated water and 4 sprigs of green mint. Add 2 oz. Old Thompson Blended Whiskey, then cubes of ice. Stir and decorate with a slice of orange and a cherry. Add a twist of lemon peel.

WHISKEY SOUR

Juice ½ Lemon
½ teaspoon Powdered Sugar
2 oz. Old Thompson
    Blended Whiskey
Shake with ice and strain into sour glass. Decorate with half-slice of lemon and a cherry.

WHISKEY SQUIRT

1½ oz. Old Thompson
    Blended Whiskey
1 tablespoon Powdered Sugar
1 tablespoon Raspberry
    Syrup or Grenadine
Shake with ice and strain into highball glass and fill with carbonated water and cubes of ice. Decorate with cubes of pineapple and strawberries.

WHISKEY SWIZZLE

Make same as Gin Swizzle (see page 64) using 2 oz. Old Thompson Blended Whiskey instead of gin.

WHISKEY TODDY (COLD)

½ teaspoon Powdered Sugar
2 teaspoons Water
2 oz. Old Thompson
    Blended Whiskey
Stir sugar and water in an old-fashioned glass. Add ice cubes and whiskey, and stir. Add a twist of lemon peel.

WHISKEY TODDY (HOT)

Put lump of sugar into hot whiskey glass and fill two-thirds with boiling water. Add 2 oz. Old Thompson Blended Whiskey. Stir and decorate with slice of lemon. Sprinkle nutmeg on top.

WHISPERS-OF-THE-FROST COCKTAIL

¾ oz. Old Thompson
  Blended Whiskey
¾ oz. Sherry
¾ oz. Port
1 teaspoon Powdered Sugar
Stir with ice and strain into cocktail glass. Serve with slices of lemon and orange.

WHITE CARGO COCKTAIL

1 small scoop Vanilla
  Ice Cream
1 oz. Old Mr. Boston Dry Gin
Shake until thoroughly mixed and add water or sauterne if the mixture is too thick. Serve in old-fashioned glass.

WHITE ELEPHANT

1½ oz. Old Mr. Boston
  Dry Gin
1 oz. Sweet Vermouth
1 Egg White
Shake with ice and strain into cocktail glass.

WHITE LADY COCKTAIL

1 Egg White
1 teaspoon Powdered Sugar
1 teaspoon Sweet Cream
1½ oz. Old Mr. Boston
  Dry Gin
Shake with ice and strain into cocktail glass.

WHITE LILY COCKTAIL

¾ oz. Old Mr. Boston
  Triple Sec
¾ oz. Old Mr. Boston Rum
¾ oz. Old Mr. Boston
  Dry Gin

¼ teaspoon Old Mr. Boston
  Anisette
Shake with ice and strain into cocktail glass.

WHITE LION COCKTAIL

Juice ½ Lemon
1 teaspoon Powdered Sugar
2 dashes Bitters
½ teaspoon Grenadine
1½ oz. Old Mr. Boston Rum
Shake with ice and strain into cocktail glass.

WHITE PLUSH

2 oz. Old Thompson
  Blended Whiskey
1 cup Milk
1 teaspoon Powdered Sugar
Shake with ice and strain into collins glass.

WHITE ROSE COCKTAIL

¾ oz. Old Mr. Boston
  Dry Gin
1 tablespoon Orange Juice
Juice 1 Lime
½ oz. Maraschino
1 Egg White
Shake with ice and strain into cocktail glass.

WHITE WAY COCKTAIL

¾ oz. Old Mr. Boston
  Crème de Menthe (White)
1½ oz. Old Mr. Boston
  Dry Gin
Shake with ice and strain into cocktail glass.

OLD Mr. BOSTON

WHY NOT?

1 oz. Old Mr. Boston Dry Gin
1 oz. Old Mr. Boston
    Apricot Flavored Brandy
½ oz. Dry Vermouth
1 dash Lemon Juice
Shake with ice and strain into cocktail glass.

WIDOW'S DREAM COCKTAIL

1½ oz. Benedictine
1 Whole Egg
Shake with ice and strain into cocktail glass. Float one teaspoon of sweet cream on top.

WIDOW'S KISS COCKTAIL

1 oz. Old Mr. Boston
    Five Star Brandy
½ oz. Chartreuse
    (Yellow)
½ oz. Benedictine
1 dash Peychaud Bitters
Shake with ice and strain into cocktail glass.

WILL ROGERS

1½ oz. Old Mr. Boston
    Dry Gin
1 tablespoon Orange Juice
½ oz. Dry Vermouth
1 dash Old Mr. Boston
    Triple Sec
Shake with ice and strain into cocktail glass.

WINDY CORNER COCKTAIL

Stir 2 oz. Old Mr. Boston Blackberry Flavored Brandy *with ice and strain into cocktail glass. Sprinkle a little nutmeg on top.*

WOODSTOCK

1½ oz. Old Mr. Boston
    Dry Gin
1 oz. Lemon Juice
1½ teaspoons Maple Syrup
1 dash Orange Bitters
Shake with ice and strain into cocktail glass.

WOODWARD COCKTAIL

1½ oz. Desmond & Duff
    Scotch Whisky
½ oz. Dry Vermouth
1 tablespoon Grapefruit Juice
Shake with ice and strain into cocktail glass.

Xanthia Cocktail

¾ oz. Old Boston Wild
Cherry Flavored Brandy
¾ oz. Chartreuse (Yellow)
¾ oz. Old Mr. Boston
Dry Gin

Stir with ice and strain into cocktail glass.

Xeres Cocktail

1 dash Orange Bitters
2 oz. Dry Sherry

Stir with ice and strain into cocktail glass.

X.Y.Z. Cocktail

1 tablespoon Lemon Juice
½ oz. Old Mr. Boston
Triple Sec
1 oz. Old Mr. Boston Rum

Shake with ice and strain into cocktail glass.

Yale Cocktail

1½ oz. Old Mr. Boston
Dry Gin
½ oz. Dry Vermouth
1 dash Bitters
1 teaspoon Blue Curacao

Stir with ice and strain into cocktail glass.

Yellow Parrot Cocktail

¾ oz. Old Mr. Boston
Anisette
¾ oz. Chartreuse (Yellow)
¾ oz. Old Mr. Boston
Apricot Flavored Brandy

Shake with ice and strain into cocktail glass.

Yellow Rattler

1 oz. Old Mr. Boston Dry Gin
1 tablespoon Orange Juice
½ oz. Dry Vermouth
½ oz. Sweet Vermouth

Shake with ice and strain into cocktail glass. Add a cocktail onion.

Yolanda

½ oz. Old Mr. Boston
Five Star Brandy
½ oz. Old Mr. Boston
Dry Gin
½ oz. Old Mr. Boston
Anisette
1 oz. Sweet Vermouth
1 dash Grenadine

Shake with ice and strain into cocktail glass. Add twist of orange peel.

Z

ZAZA COCKTAIL

1½ oz. Old Mr. Boston
    Dry Gin
¾ oz. Dubonnet

Stir with ice and strain into cocktail glass. Add a twist of orange peel.

ZERO MINT

For each serving chill 2 oz. Old Mr. Boston Crème de Menthe (Green) mixed with 1 oz. water in freezing compartment of refrigerator for 2 hours or longer if desired. (Does not have to be frozen solid.) Serve in cocktail glasses.

ZOMBIE

1 oz. Unsweetened Pineapple
    Juice
Juice 1 Lime
Juice 1 Small Orange
1 teaspoon Powdered Sugar
½ oz. Old Mr. Boston
    Apricot Flavored Brandy
2½ oz. Old Mr. Boston Rum
1 oz. Jamaica Rum
1 oz. Passion Fruit Syrup
    (if desired)

Put all ingredients with half a cup of crushed ice into a blender. Blend at low speed for a minute and strain into frosted zombie glass. Decorate with stick of pineapple and one green and one red cherry.

Carefully float ½ oz. 151 Proof Rum and then top with sprig of fresh mint dipped in powdered sugar. Serve with straw.

Special Sections

Egg Nog

Sᴏᴍᴇ ᴘᴇᴏᴘʟᴇ ʙᴇʟɪᴇᴠᴇ that this name is of English derivation and that "nog" comes from the word "noggin," a small drinking vessel with an upright handle. On the other hand, there are those who believe that the name is a result of joining the sounds of egg 'n grog. From whatever source, the drink itself is American dating back to about 1775. In the early days, eggnog was associated with traveling and social functions.

Traditionally, the liquors used in eggnog have been rum and brandy. However, whiskey, sherry, ale, and cider may be used. Some of the early recipes called for milking the cow into the liquor but today, fortunately, this is unnecessary as simpler methods are now available. There are excellent nonalcoholic, prepared eggnogs to which one's favorite liquor may be added. These are available during the holiday season from virtually all dairy companies. Most of the following are simplified versions of recipes listed alphabetically in this book (for those who prefer to make their own preparations). For a complete list of recipes see the Index, page *203*.

Mɪxɪɴɢ Iɴꜱᴛʀᴜᴄᴛɪᴏɴꜱ

A smaller or greater quantity of liquor than that called for in the following recipes may be used, depending on one's preference. Best results are obtained when all ingredients have been prechilled. Stir well, sprinkle nutmeg on top, and serve in 4 oz. punch cups or glasses.

AMBASSADOR'S MORNING LIFT

1 qt. Prepared Dairy Eggnog
6 oz. Remy Martin Cognac
3 oz. Jamaica Rum
3 oz. Mr. Boston Crème
    de Cacao (Brown)
Mr. Boston Five Star Brandy
or **Kentucky Tavern Bourbon Whiskey** *may be substituted for Cognac.*

BALTIMORE EGGNOG

1 qt. Prepared Dairy Eggnog
5 oz. Old Mr. Boston Five
    Star Brandy
5 oz. Jamaica Rum
5 oz. Madeira Wine

BRANDY EGGNOG

1 qt. Prepared Dairy Eggnog
12 oz. Old Mr. Boston Five
    Star Brandy

BREAKFAST EGGNOG

1 qt. Prepared Dairy Eggnog
10 oz. Old Mr. Boston
    Apricot Flavored Brandy
2½ oz. Old Mr. Boston
    Triple Sec

CHRISTMAS YULE EGGNOG

1 qt. Prepared Dairy Eggnog
12 oz. Old Thompson
    Blended Whiskey
1½ oz. Old Mr. Boston Rum

GENERAL HARRISON'S EGGNOG

1 qt. Prepared Dairy Eggnog
24 oz. Sweet Cider

IMPERIAL EGGNOG

1 qt. Prepared Dairy Eggnog
10 oz. Old Mr. Boston
    Five Star Brandy
2 oz. Old Mr. Boston
    Apricot Flavored Brandy

NASHVILLE EGGNOG

1 qt. Prepared Dairy Eggnog
6 oz. Kentucky Tavern
    Bourbon Whiskey
3 oz. Old Mr. Boston
    Five Star Brandy
3 oz. Jamaica Rum

PORT WINE EGGNOG

1 qt. Prepared Dairy Eggnog
18 oz. Port Wine

RUM EGGNOG

1 qt. Prepared Dairy Eggnog
12 oz. Old Mr. Boston Rum

SHERRY EGGNOG

1 qt. Prepared Dairy Eggnog
18 oz. Sherry Wine

WHISKEY EGGNOG

1 qt. Prepared Dairy Eggnog
12 oz. Old Thompson
    Blended Whiskey

The Martini

THOUGH THE MARTINI is viewed with almost reverent awe as a drink of unique power, it is no more or less powerful than any other drink containing the same amount of alcohol.

The original Martini recipe called for one-half dry gin and one-half dry vermouth. This proportion began to change in the early 1940s to two or three parts dry gin to one part dry vermouth. Today, popular proportions for an Extra Dry Martini range from 5-to-1 to an 8-to-1 ratio. The greater the proportion of gin to vermouth, the "drier" the Martini.

ARE YOUR MARTINIS TOO STRONG?

Remember, America is nearly the only country in the world that drinks high-proof gin. The British, who perfected gin, and the Canadians prefer their gin at milder, smoother 80 proof.

To make Martinis that are extra dry but not extra strong, use 80 proof gin. The chart below shows how the trend to drier Martinis has increased the alcoholic content of this popular drink from a smooth 76.5 proof to a powerful 84 proof! Today's very dry Martini can be returned to its original, more moderate proof only by using 80 proof gin.

Using Standard 36 Proof Dry Vermouth	With 90 Proof Dry Gin	Or 80 Proof Dry Gin (or Vodka)
3–to–1 (Traditional)	76.5 Proof	69.0 Proof
5–to–1 (Dry)	81.0 Proof	72.6 Proof
8–to–1 (Extra Dry)	84.0 Proof	75.1 Proof

MARTINI MIXING

Chill 3-ounce cocktail glasses to the point of frost. Fill Martini pitcher with cracked (not crushed) ice. Ice should be dry and hard frozen. Measure out the exact ingredients for

◄ *Mr. Boston Mai Tai Cocktail—25 Proof*
Mr. Boston Vodka Martini Cocktail—40 Proof

the number of drinks required, pouring in the dry gin first (gin should "smoke" as it settles over the cold ice), then the Dry Vermouth. Stir briskly until drink is very cold. Strain at once into frosty, stemmed cocktail glasses. For Martinis "on the rocks," use prechilled Old-Fashioned glasses and pour the liquor over cubes of ice. A twist of lemon peel adds a special character to a Martini which many prefer.

The following are the more popular Martinis.

MARTINI
(Traditional 2-to-1)
1½ oz. Old Mr. Boston
    Dry Gin
¾ oz. Dry Vermouth
Serve with an olive.

DRY MARTINI
(5-to-1)
1⅔ oz. Old Mr. Boston
    Dry Gin
⅓ oz. Dry Vermouth
Serve with an olive.

EXTRA DRY MARTINI
(8-to-1)
2 oz. Old Mr. Boston Dry Gin
¼ oz. Dry Vermouth
Serve with an olive.

MARTINI (Sweet)
1 oz. Old Mr. Boston
    Dry Gin
1 oz. Sweet Vermouth
Serve with an olive.

VODKA MARTINI
Substitute Old Mr. Boston Vodka *for* Old Mr. Boston Dry Gin *in any of these Martini recipes.*

MARTINI (Medium)
1½ oz. Old Mr. Boston
    Dry Gin
½ oz. Dry Vermouth
½ oz. Sweet Vermouth
Serve with an olive.

BOSTON BULLET
A Martini substituting an olive stuffed with an almond for the regular olive.

DILLATINI
A Martini substituting a Dilly Bean in place of the olive.

GIBSON
This is a Dry or Extra Dry Martini with a twist of lemon peel and served with one to three pearl onions. May also be made with Old Mr. Boston Vodka.

TEQUINI
A Martini made with Tequila instead of dry gin. Serve with a twist of lemon peel and an olive.

Bar Hints and Measurements

HERE ARE SOME SUGGESTIONS and fine points that will help you mix a perfect drink every time. Follow them carefully and your drinks will have the extra added touch of artistry that will mark you as a professional.

EQUIPMENT

Here is a sensible list of basic, serviceable items for even the most professional bar.

- A jigger measure—designed with an accurate scale of half and quarter ounces
- A sturdy mixing glass or shaker
- A bar strainer
- A teaspoon or set of measuring spoons
- A glass stirring rod, or a long spoon—for mixing and stirring
- A corkscrew, can and bottle opener
- A paring knife—for paring and cutting fruit
- A vacuum-type ice bucket with tongs
- A wooden muddler—for mashing mint, herbs, fruits
- A lemon-lime squeezer
- A large pitcher—with a good pouring lip
- A variety of glassware

A Buying Guide

Use the following as a reference for determining approximately how many bottles you may need for various occasions. Fifths may be used in place of metric 750 ml bottles. To be extra safe, but conservative, substitute liters or quarts for the above sizes.

No. of People	For Cock- tails	You'll Need at Least	For Buffet or Dinner	You'll Need at Least	For an After- Dinner Party	You'll Need at Least
4	10 to 16 drinks	1-750 ml	8 cocktails	1-750 ml	12 to 16 drinks	1-750 ml
			8 glasses wine	2 bottles		
			4 liqueurs	1-500 ml		
			8 highballs	1-750 ml		
6	15 to 22 drinks	2-750 mls	12 cocktails	1-750 ml	18 to 26 drinks	2-750 mls
			12 glasses wine	2 bottles		
			8 liqueurs	1-750 ml		
			18 highballs	2-750 mls		
8	18 to 24 drinks	2-750 mls	16 cocktails	1-750 ml	20 to 34 drinks	2-750 mls
			16 glasses wine	3 bottles		
			10 liqueurs	1-750 ml		
			18 highballs	2-750 mls		
12	20 to 40 drinks	3-750 mls	24 cocktails	2-750 mls	25 to 45 drinks	3-750 mls
			24 glasses wine	4 bottles		
			16 liqueurs	1-750 ml		
			30 highballs	3-750 mls		
20	40 to 65 drinks	4-750 mls	40 cocktails	3-750 mls	45 to 75 drinks	5-750 mls
			40 glasses wine	7 bottles		
			25 liqueurs	2-750 mls		
			50 highballs	4-750 mls		

Measuring

Even the most professional bartender measures the ingredients of every drink, even though experience may permit some to do this by eye and by skillful freehand pouring. However, to make a perfect drink every time, measure all ingredients. Remember, too, that many drinks can be spoiled by being too strong as well as too weak.

Some standard bar measures:

1 Dash	1/6 teaspoon (1/32 ounce)
1 Teaspoon (bar spoon)	1/8 ounce
1 Tablespoon	3/8 ounce
1 Pony	1 ounce
1 Jigger (barglass)	1-1/2 ounces
1 Wineglass	4 ounces
1 Split	6 ounces
1 Cup	8 ounces

METRIC STANDARDS OF FILL FOR DISTILLED SPIRITS

Metric Size	Fluid Ounces	Nearest U.S. Equivalent	Fluid Ounces	Number of Bottles per Case
50 ml.	1.7	miniature	1.6	120
200 ml.	6.8	1/2 pint	8	48
500 ml.	16.9	1 pint	16	24
750 ml.	25.4	4/5 quart	25.6	12
1 liter	33.8	1 quart	32	12
1.75 liters	59.2	1/2 gallon	64	6

METRIC SIZES FOR WINE

Name of Package	New Metric Size	New Metric Fluid Oz.	Bottles Per Case
Split	187 ml.	6.34	48
Tenth	375 ml.	12.68	24
Fifth	750 ml.	25.36	12
Quart	1 liter	33.81	12
Magnum	1.5 liters	50.72	6
Jeroboam	3 liters	101.44	4

ml. = milliliters   1 liter = 1,000 milliliters

LIQUID MEASURES

	Metric and United States Equivalents	
Metric Units	U.S. Unit	Metric Unit
10 milliliters = 1 centiliter	1 fluid ounce =	29.573 milliliters
10 centiliters = 1 deciliter		
10 deciliters = 1 liter	1 quart =	9.4635 deciliters 0.94635 liter
10 liters = 1 decaliter		
10 decaliters = 1 hectoliter	1 gallon =	3.7854 liters
10 hectoliters = 1 kiloliter	0.033814 fluid ounce = 1 milliliter	
	3.3814 fluid ounces = 1 deciliter	
	33.814 fluid ounces 1.0567 quarts 0.26417 gallon	= 1 liter

GLASSWARE

All recipes in this book indicate the type of glass that is appropriate for each drink.

Always use clean sparkling glassware. Keep one towel for drying and another for polishing. A stemmed glass should be used for cocktails served without ice, so that the heat of the hand holding the glass will not warm the drink as it is being consumed.

How to Chill a Glass

Cocktail glasses should be well chilled to keep the drinks refreshingly cold. If refrigerator space is not available for prechilling, fill each glass with cracked, shaved, or crushed ice before mixing. When the drink is ready, empty the glass, shake out the melted ice, and then pour the drink.

How to Frost a Glass

There are two types of "frosted" glass. For "frosted" drinks, glasses should be stored in a refrigerator or buried in shaved ice long enough to give each glass a white, frosted, ice-cold look and feel.

For a "sugar-frosted" glass, moisten the rim of a prechilled glass with a slice of lime or lemon and then dip the rim into powdered sugar.

Ice

Use plenty of ice. Whether cubed, cracked, crushed, or shaved, all ice should be fresh, crystal-clear, and free of any taste. Always put ice in the mixing glass, shaker, or drinking glass before pouring any ingredients. The liquids are chilled as they are poured over the ice and there is no splashing.

Most highballs, Old Fashioneds, and on-the-rocks drinks call for ice cubes. Use cracked or cubed ice for stirring and shaking; crushed or shaved ice for special tall drinks, frappés, and other drinks to be sipped through straws.

Sugar

Always place sugar in the mixing glass before adding the liquor. Unless otherwise stated in the recipe, powdered sugar should be used with alcohol. Powdered sugar dissolves and blends quickest with alcohol at low temperatures.

Simple syrup may be substituted for powdered sugar in many drinks. Some bartenders claim it gives certain drinks a smoother, richer taste. Many prefer it because it blends instantly. You may make a simple syrup ahead of time and store it in bottles in a cool place. Dissolve one pound of granulated sugar in one-half pint of warm water, gradually stirring in enough water to make one pint of syrup.

WHEN TO STIR

Drinks containing clear liquors and ingredients require stirring with ice for proper mixing. Stir drinks containing a carbonated mixer (tonic water, ginger ale, cola, etc.) *gently* to preserve the sparkle and effervescence. Remember, too little stirring fails to mix or chill the ingredients; too much stirring melts the ice and dilutes the drink.

WHEN TO SHAKE

Drinks containing fruit juices, sugar, eggs, cream, or other ingredients difficult to mix, should be shaken briskly. For thorough blending of some punches, sours, and other fruit and egg drinks, and where frothiness is desired, use an electric mixer or blender.

USING THE STRAINER

Strain all cocktails before serving with a wire—not silver—strainer. Use one with clips that permits the wire to rest within the rim of the mixing glass or shaker.

POURING

When mixing the same cocktail for four or more people, make the drinks in one batch. To make each drink of equal strength and taste, set up the required number of glasses in a row. Pour, filling each glass only halfway. Then go back to the first glass and finish off.

HOW TO FLOAT CORDIALS

To make cordials or brandy float one on top of the other in the same glass, as in the Pousse Café, pour each ingredient slowly over a teaspoon held bottom side up over the glass. The rounded surface of the teaspoon will spread each cordial or brandy slowly and evenly over the one below without mixing. This may also be accomplished by first inserting a glass stirring rod into the glass and then slowly pouring each ingredient down the rod.

Be sure to pour all ingredients in the order given in the recipe.

How to Flame Liquor

The secret to setting liquor (brandy, rum, gin, whiskey) aflame in drink and cooking recipes is to make certain that the glass, cooking vessel, and liquor are all prewarmed. Start with a teaspoon or tablespoon of liquor, preheat over flame, then set afire. Pour flaming liquid carefully into remaining liquor to be set aflame.

Using Eggs

To separate the white of an egg from the yellow, break the egg by hitting the center on the edge of a glass. Separate the two halves, passing the yolk from one half-shell to the other until the white slips through to the glass below.

The egg always goes into the mixing glass or shaker before the liquor, to make certain that the egg is fresh. When shaking, use cubed or cracked ice to break up and blend the egg with the other ingredients.

Using Fruit and Fruit Juices

Whenever possible use only *fresh* fruit. Wash the outside peel before using. Fruit slices should be cut about one-quarter-inch thick and slit toward the center to fix slice on rim of glass. Keep garnishes fresh and cold.

When mixing drinks containing fruit juices, *always* pour the liquor last. Squeeze and strain fruit juices just before using to insure freshness and good taste. Avoid artificial, concentrated substitutes.

Twist of Lemon Peel

When recipes call for a twist of lemon peel, rub a narrow strip of peel around the rim of the glass to deposit the oil on it. Then twist the peel so that the oil (usually one small drop) will drop into the drink. Then drop in the peel. The lemon oil gives added character to the cocktail which many prefer.

USING BITTERS

Ordinarily, only a dash or two is necessary. This small but important ingredient can add zest to a great number of mixed drinks. Made from numerous and subtle combinations of roots, barks, berries, and herbs, they are all characterized by their aromatic, bitter taste.

Here are a few of the best-known brands:

Angostura Bitters—made in Trinidad from an ancient, secret recipe.

Abbott's Aged Bitters—made in Baltimore by the same family since 1865.

Peychaud's Bitters—made in New Orleans.

Orange Bitters—made from the dried peel of bitter Seville oranges and sold by several English firms.

VERMOUTH

Vermouth is a white appetizer wine flavored with as many as thirty to forty different herbs, roots, berries, flowers and seeds. There are nearly as many vermouth formulas as there are brand labels.

The dry variety (French) is light gold in color and has a delightful nutty flavor. Sweet (Italian) vermouth is richer in flavor and more syrupy. Both are delicate and will lose their freshness if left too long in an opened bottle. Use with care and discretion in mixed drinks (follow the recipe) since most people now prefer "drier" cocktails.

The Liquor Dictionary

Much of the enjoyment of social drinking comes from a knowledge of the different types of alcoholic beverages available. This section was prepared to help you understand some of the ofttimes subtle differences between one type of liquor and another.

First, here are a few common terms frequently misunderstood.

Alcohol (C_2H_5OH) the common ingredient of all liquor. There are many types of alcohol, but for beverages only ethyl alcohol is used. Of the several types of ethyl alcohol, those spirits distilled from grain, grape, fruit, and cane are the most common.

Proof—a measurement of alcoholic strength or content. One degree of proof equals one-half of 1 percent of alcohol. An 80 proof product contains 40 percent alcohol; a 90 proof product, 45 percent alcohol, etc.

For centuries Scotch, British Gin, and Canadian Whisky sold in England, Scotland, Canada and most of the rest of the world has been sold at mild 80 proof. America has only begun to appreciate the tasteful qualities of the more moderate lower proofs.

In recent years, a trend has developed in this country toward 80 proof blended and straight whiskies, dry gin, Scotch, and Canadian whiskies. Practically all of the rum sold in America is now 80 proof. Vodka at 80 proof outsells the higher proofs 9-to-1. For years the most expensive, famous-name Cognacs have been imported at 80 proof, and now nearly all American-made brandy is 80 proof.

Age—often believed to be the *only* indications of quality; a whiskey, rum, or brandy can be aged too long as well as not long enough. Other factors affecting quality include variables in the distilling process itself, the types of grain used, the warehousing techniques employed, the rate of aging, and the degree of skill used in determining product maturity. Aging may make good whiskey better, but no amount of aging can make good whiskey out of bad.

GRAIN NEUTRAL SPIRITS—a practically tasteless, colorless, alcohol distilled from grain (like whiskey) but at 190 proof or above, whereas whiskey must be distilled at less than 190 proof. Used in blended whiskies, in making gin and vodka, and in many other liquors.

WINE—produced principally from the fermented juice of grapes. If any other fruit is used, the name of the fruit must appear on the label. The alcoholic content of wine ranges from less than 14 percent to 21 percent.

BEER—the name for five types of fermented malt beverages: *Lager Beer* (about 3.6 precent alcohol), the most popular type of light, dry beer; *Ale,* having a more pronounced flavor and aroma of hops, is heavier and more bitter than lager beer; *Bock Beer, Porter,* and *Stout* (about 6 percent alcohol), which are progressively heavier, darker, richer, and sweeter than either lager beer or ale.

Brandy

Brandy is distilled from a fermented mash of grapes or other fruit. These brandies, aged in oak casks, are usually bottled at 80 proof. Long enjoyed as an after dinner drink, brandy is also widely used in cooking.

Cognac—this fine brandy, known for its smoothness and heady dry aroma, is produced only in the Cognac region of France. (All Cognac is brandy, but not all brandy is Cognac, nor is all French brandy Cognac.)

Armagnac—is much like Cognac but has a drier taste. It is produced only in the Armagnac region of France.

American Brandy—all of which is distilled in California, has its own excellent characteristics of taste. Unlike European brandies (whose farmer-distillers sell their brandies to blender-shippers who control the brand names), California brandies are usually produced by individual firms that grow the grapes, distill, age, blend, bottle, and market the brandies under their own brand names.

Apple Brandy, Apple Jack, or Calvados—is distilled from a cider made from apples. Calvados is produced only in Normandy, France. Apple Jack may be bottled-in-bond under the same regulations that apply to whiskey.

Fruit-flavored Brandies—are brandy-based liqueurs produced from blackberries, peaches, apricots, cherries, and ginger. They are usually bottled at 70 or 80 proof.

Cordials

THE WORDS *cordial* and *liqueur* are synonymous, describing liquors made by mixing or redistilling neutral spirits with fruits, flowers, herbs, seeds, roots, plants, or juices to which sweetening has been added. Practically all cordials are sweet and colorful, with highly concentrated, dessertlike flavor.

Cordials are made in all countries. Several, made from closely guarded secret recipes and processes, are known throughout the world by their trade or proprietary brand names.

Here are brief descriptions of the cordials and flavoring mentioned most frequently in the recipes in this book:

ABSINTHE—anise seed (licorice) flavor; contains wormwood; illegal in the United States

ABSINTHE SUBSTITUTES—Abisante, Abson, Anisette, Herbsaint, Mistra, Ojen, Oxygene, Pernod

AMARETTO DI SARONNO—the original Italian almond flavored liqueur

AMER PICON—bitter, orange-flavored French cordial made from quinine and spices

ANISETTE—anise seed, licorice flavor

BENEDICTINE—secret herb formula first produced by Benedictine monks

BITTERS—(see page 181)

CHARTREUSE—yellow and green herb liqueurs developed by Carthusian monks

CREME(S)—so-called because high sugar content results in cream-like consistency

CRÈME DE CACAO—from cacao and vanilla beans

CRÈME DE CASSIS—from black currants

CRÈME DE MENTHE—from mint

CRÈME DE NOYAUX—from almonds

CURACAO—orange-flavored, made of dried orange peel, from Dutch West Indies

DUBONNET—French aperitif wine made from aromatics, has slight quinine taste

FORBIDDEN FRUIT—a domestic liqueur produced by blending shaddock fruit (a type of grapefruit) and imported Cognac

GRENADINE—made from pomegranates, used for flavoring

KÜMMEL—caraway and anise seeds and other herb flavors

MARASCHINO—liqueur made from cherries grown in Dalmatia, Yugoslavia

PASSION FRUIT (PASSIONOLA)—a nonalcoholic mix made from the Passion Flower

PEPPERMINT SCHNAPPS—a light-bodied crème de menthe

PERNOD—a French anise-flavored liqueur and absinthe substitute

ROCK AND RYE—fruit juice, rock candy, and rye whiskey, bottled with fruit slices

SLOE GIN—a liqueur made from sloe berries (blackthorn bush)

SWEDISH PUNCH—Scandinavian liqueur made from Batavia Arak rum, tea, lemon, and other spices. Also known as Arrack Punsch and Caloric Punsch (the latter because it gives off heat)

TRIPLE SEC—colorless Curacao, but less sweet.

Gin

GIN, which is distilled from grain, receives its flavor and aroma from juniper berries and other botanicals. (Every gin producer has his own special recipe.)

Most gin is colorless, though some brands may be golden or straw-yellow because of aging in barrels. Even though a distiller ages his gin, he cannot, by law, make age claims for his product. Gin sold around the world at 80 proof is bottled in this country at proofs varying from 80 to 94.

DRY GIN—merely signifies that the gin lacks sweetness.

VACUUM-DISTILLED GIN—is distilled in a glass-lined vacuum still at a low 90° Fahrenheit temperature (instead of at the usual 212°), capturing only the light, volatile flavors and aromas without the bitterness found in some gins.

LONDON DRY GIN—originated in England and is now considered a generic term and may appear on American-made gins as well. Dry gins from England are inclined to be a little heavier-bodied.

GOLDEN GIN—is a dry gin which, due to aging in wood, has acquired a golden color.

HOLLAND, GENEVA, OR SCHIEDAM GINS—are imported from Holland, where gin originated, and are highly flavored and rich in aromatic oils; they do not mix well with other ingredients in cocktails.

OLD TOM GIN—is an English gin that has been sweetened with sugar syrup.

FLAVORED GIN—is a sweet gin usually flavored with orange, lemon, or mint.

SLOE GIN—is not a gin at all but a liqueur. (See page *186*.)

Rum

Rum is distilled from the fermented juice of sugar cane, cane syrup, and molasses at less than 190 proof (160 proof for New England rum) and bottled at not less than 80 proof. It is aged in uncharred barrels where it picks up very little coloring; dark rums often have caramel added to them for color.

Most rums are blends of several aged rums, ranging from heavy, pungent types to light, brandylike varieties; selected for special aroma, flavor, and color. There are two main types of rum:

LIGHT-BODIED RUMS—are dry with only a very slight molasses flavor. Available in two varieties, White and Gold Label (or Light and Dark), the Gold or Dark is usually a bit sweeter with a more pronounced taste. Among these rums are included rums from Puerto Rico, Cuba, and the Virgin Islands. Light-bodied rums are also produced in the Dominican Republic, Haiti, Venezuela, Mexico, Hawaii, and the Philippines.

HEAVY-BODIED RUMS—are darker and sweeter and have a pungent bouquet, body, and flavor. These are distilled by a different and slower fermentation process, which allows more time for a fuller, richer molasses-like body to develop and include rums from Jamaica, Demerara (British Guiana), Martinique, Trinidad, Barbados, and New England.

Vodka

VODKA, most versatile of all alcoholic beverages, is a highly refined and filtered liquor distilled at or above 190 proof, bottled at not less than 80 or more than 110 proof. It was originally made in Russia, from potatoes, but in the United States, vodka is usually distilled from grain, primarily corn and wheat. The subtle differences between various vodkas results from the types of grain used and the distilling and filtering processes employed. Most American vodkas are filtered through activated charcoal.

Vodka is not aged; it is colorless and virtually tasteless and odorless. In Russia and the Baltic countries, vodka is always taken straight and ice-cold from small glasses, at one swallow, along with food. In America, vodka is usually mixed with fruit juices, carbonated beverages, and other ingredients where vodka's softness and palatability does not interfere with the taste of the main ingredient, although vodka martinis are becoming increasingly popular.

FLAVORED VODKA—an American-originated product. Excellent straight or in mixed drinks, it has been sweetened and flavored, usually with orange, lemon, lime, mint, or grape. It is usually bottled at 70 proof.

ZUBROVKA—a Polish vodka in which a bit of special "buffalo" grass is steeped. This European grass gives the vodka a light yellowish color and a slight aromatic bouquet. It can be made at home by buying "buffalo" grass from an herb company and steeping it in vodka.

Whiskey

Whiskies are distilled from a fermented mash of grain (usually corn, rye, barley, or wheat), and then aged in oak barrels. In this country, whiskey must be distilled at less than 190 proof (although whiskey with a special designation such as Bourbon, Rye, etc., cannot be distilled above 160 proof) and must be bottled at no less than 80 proof.

Whiskey, when placed in barrels to age, is a water-colored liquid. It is during the aging period that whiskey obtains its characteristic amber color, flavor, and aroma.

The major whiskey-producing countries are the United States, Canada, Scotland and Ireland. Special grain characteristics, recipes and distillation processes make the whiskey of each country distinct from that of the others.

AMERICAN WHISKEY—Although American whiskies fall into three major categories, straight whiskey, light whiskey, and blended whiskey, the United States government acknowledges thirty-three distinct types of whiskey. Only the major types (98 percent of the nation's consumption) are covered here.

Straight Whiskey is distilled from corn, rye, barley or wheat (not blended with neutral grain spirits or any other whiskey) and aged in charred oak barrels for a minimum of two years. There are four major types of straight whiskey:

1. *Bourbon Whiskey* is distilled from a mash of grain containing not less than 51 percent corn and is normally aged four years in new charred oak barrels. Bourbon is amber in color and full-bodied in flavor. When distilled in Kentucky it is usually referred to as *Kentucky Straight Bourbon Whiskey*. Bourbon is named for Bourbon County in Kentucky where this

type of whiskey originated. Bourbon is also produced in Illinois, Indiana, Ohio, Pennsylvania, Tennessee and Missouri.

2. *Rye Whiskey* is distilled from a mash of grain containing not less than 51 percent rye and is much like bourbon in color, but it is different in taste and heavier in flavor.

3. *Corn Whiskey is* distilled from a mash of grain containing not less than 80 per cent corn. Corn whiskey is commonly aged in re-used charred oak barrels.

4. *Bottled-in-Bond Whiskey* is straight whiskey, usually bourbon or rye, which is produced under United States government supervision. Though the government does not guarantee the quality of bonded whiskey, it does require that the whiskey be at least four years old, that it be bottled at 100 proof, that it be produced in one distilling by the same distiller, and that it be sorted and bottled at a bonded warehouse under government supervision.

Light Whiskey is a new type of American whiskey which is produced at between 160 proof and 189 proof and stored in used, charred oak containers for a minimum of four years. Significant characteristics are the lightness of flavor and smoothness of taste. Color, which may vary from clear to amber, is not significant.

Blended Whiskey—A blend of one or more straight whiskies and neutral grain spirits containing at least 20 percent or more straight whiskey bottled at not less than 80 proof.

1. *Kentucky Whiskey— A Blend* is a blended whiskey in which all the straight bottled whiskies are distilled in Kentucky.

2. *A Blend of Straight Whiskies* occurs when two or more straight whiskies are blended together, to the exclusion of neutral grain spirits.

3. *American Blended Light Whiskey* is a new American whiskey category consisting of less than 20 percent of straight whiskies, at 100 proof, and more than 80 percent of American light whiskey.

CANADIAN WHISKY—Canadian whiskies are blended whiskies, usually distilled from rye, corn, and barley. Produced only in Canada, under government supervision, most of the Canadian whisky sold in this country is at least four years old. Canadian whisky, usually lighter bodied than American whiskey, is sold in Canada, and in most of the world, except the United States, at 80 proof.

SCOTCH WHISKY—Produced only in Scotland, Scotch whiskies are blended whiskies deriving their individual personalities from native barley grain and traditional pot stills. All Scotch blends contain malt whisky and grain whisky (similar to American grain neutral spirits). Scotch's distinctive smoky flavor comes from drying malted barley over peat fires. All the Scotch imported into this country is at least four years old and is usually 80 or 86 proof. Scotch sold in the rest of the world is almost always 80 proof.

IRISH WHISKY—Produced only in Ireland, Irish whisky, like Scotch, is a blended whisky containing both barley malt whiskies and grain whiskies. Unlike Scotch, however, the malt is dried in coal-fired kilns and the aroma of the fires does not reach the malt. Irish whisky is heavier and more full-bodied than Scotch and is usually 86 proof.

Index

If you know the name of the mixed drink you desire, you need not use this index, as all drinks are listed alphabetically throughout the book.

This index is arranged so that you may choose specific types of drinks such as cocktails, fizzes, highballs, etc., or cocktails made with Gin, Vodka, Whiskey, Sloe Gin, and other ingredients.

ADES

These are perfect warm-weather drinks, served tall and frosty with plenty of ice and garnished with slices of fruit. They are made primarily with sweetened lemon or lime juice and a variety of liquors and may be filled with plain or soda water.

AMARETTO DRINKS

AMER PICON DRINKS

ANISETTE DRINKS

APPLE BRANDY DRINKS

APPLEJACK DRINKS

APRICOT BRANDY DRINKS

BEER DRINKS

BENEDICTINE DRINKS

BLACKBERRY BRANDY DRINKS

BRANDY DRINKS

CHAMPAGNE DRINKS

CHARTREUSE DRINKS
(Green)

CHARTREUSE DRINKS
(Yellow)

CHERRY BRANDY DRINKS

CHERRY VODKA DRINKS

CHERRY WINE DRINKS

COBBLERS

These tall drinks are generally served in a large goblet. They are made with lots of shaved ice, fruit, and liquor, decorated with berries, fresh fruit, and if desired, a sprig of mint. Served with straws.

COFFEE BRANDY DRINKS

COFFEE LIQUEUR DRINKS

COGNAC DRINKS

COLLINS

These are tall, cool drinks belonging to the punch family, with Tom and John the best known members. Any basic liquor can be used, with the juice of lemon or lime, poured over ice cubes in a frosted 12-oz. highball glass. Add sugar to taste and fill with soda water. Garnish with a slice of lemon and a cherry.

Apricot Anise Collins 7
Brandy Collins 20
Gables Collins 60
John Collins 81
Mint Collins 96
Rum Collins 125
Sloe Gin Collins 137
Tequila Collins 144
Tom Collins 150
Victory Collins 156
Vodka Collins 156
Whiskey Collins 161

COOLERS

A cooler is a tall, warm-weather drink not unlike an individual punch except that less lemon or lime juice is used in a cooler (usually just fruit rinds). They are made with different types of liquor, flavoring, cracked ice, and a carbonated beverage.

Apricot Cooler 7
Boston Cooler 19
Cherry Cooler 36
Country Club Cooler 44
Floradora Cooler 56
Gin Cooler 63
Harvard Cooler 71
Highland Cooler 73
Klondike Cooler 83
Lone Tree Cooler 90
Pike's Peak Cooler 111
Pineapple Cooler 111
Remsen Cooler 121
Robert E. Lee Cooler 122
Rock and Rye Cooler 122
Rum Cooler 126
Saratoga Cooler 130
Scotch Cooler 131
Vodka Cooler 158

CRÈME D'ALMOND DRINKS

Gables Collins 60
Mikado Cocktail 96
Pink Squirrel Cocktail 113

CRÈME DE BANANA DRINKS

Banshee 11
Boston Gold 19
Capri 32
Caribbean Champagne 34
Hyatt's Jamaican Banana 76
La Jolla 85
Top Banana 150
West Indian Punch 160

CRÈME DE CACAO DRINKS
(Brown)

Ambassador's Morning Lift 171
Barbary Coast 11
Caledonia 30
Chocolate Rum 38
Fifth Avenue 55
Fox River 57
Panama Cocktail 107
Toreador 150
Velvet Hammer No. 1 155

CRÈME DE CACAO
(White)

Alexander No. 1 2
Alexander No. 2 2
Angel's Kiss 5
Angel's Tip 5
Angel's Wing 6
Aunt Jemima 9
Banshee 11
Barnaby's Buffalo Blizzard 11
Capri 32
Cole's Raspberry Dream 42
Eye-Opener 53
Flying Grasshopper 56
Golden Cadillac 67
Grasshopper 68
Hyatt's Jamaican Banana 76
Jamaica Hop 79
Jockey Club 80
Kretchma Cocktail 83
Maxim Cocktail 94
Mocha Mint 98
Ninotchka Cocktail 103
Peach Bunny 110
Peppermint Pattie 110
Peppermint Stick 110
Pink Squirrel Cocktail 113
Robin's Nest 122
Russian Bear 127
Russian Cocktail 128
Savannah 130
Tropical Cocktail 151
Velvet Hammer No. 2 155
Vodka Grasshopper 158

CRÈME DE CASSIS DRINKS

Brandy Cassis 20
Kir Cocktail 82
Parisian 109
Pousse Café 116
Vermouth Cassis 155

Cups

These delectable wine cocktails are made with brandy and Triple Sec mixed with sweet wine, dry champagne, or cider. Make in glass pitchers with ice cubes and serve in stemmed claret glasses.

Curacao Drinks

Crème de Menthe Drinks
(Green)

Crème de Menthe Drinks
(White)

DAISIES

These overgrown cocktails are made of liquor, grenadine (or other cordials), and lemon or lime juice. Usually shaken with cracked ice, they are served in stein, metal cup, or old-fashioned glass over an ice cube and decorated with fruit.

DRY GIN DRINKS

DUBONNET DRINKS

EGGNOGS

This is a most agreeable, enriching way of taking whole eggs and milk. They can be served in cups, from a bowl, or in a tall, individually prepared glass. In any case, a sprinkling of nutmeg is a must.

FIXES

These sweet "miniature" cobblers are made in highball glasses with liquor, lemon juice, sugar and lots of shaved ice. Serve with fruits, berries, and straws.

FIZZES

An early-morning, midafternoon, or evening pleasure, these are made from liquor, citrus juices, and sugar, shaken with ice and strained into small highball glasses, which are then filled with "fizz" (soda) water, though different carbonated beverages, even champagne, may be used. A few call for egg whites or yolks.

FLIPS

This combination eggnog and fizz is made with liquor, egg and sugar, shaken well with cracked ice and strained into short stemmed flip glasses. Good early morning or bedtime drinks, sprinkled with nutmeg.

GALLIANO DRINKS

HIGHBALLS

These are all-time favorites and simple to make. Practically any liquor may be used, in combination with ice, soda or plain water, ginger ale, and a host of other carbonated liquids.

HOT DRINKS

Made right and served piping hot, these are fine drinks for snappy days and cold evenings. Don't use too much liquor in any hot drink; if it's too strong it can't be taken until it cools and then it's no good.

IRISH WHISKY DRINKS

RICKEYS

A cross between a collins and a sour, they are always made with lime, cracked ice, soda water, or some other carbonated beverage. The liquor may be whiskey, gin, rum, or brandy. Serve with the rind of the lime left in the glass.

ROCK & RYE DRINKS

RUM DRINKS

SANGAREES

These are taller, sweet old fashioneds (without bitters); they may be made with whiskey, gin, rum, or brandy, with port wine floated on top, or with wine, ale, porter, or stout, with a sprinkle of nutmeg.

SCOTCH WHISKY DRINKS

SLINGS

These are like sangarees, but made with the addition of lemon juice and a twist of lemon peel. Usually served in an old fashioned glass.

SLOE GIN DRINKS

SMASHES

These are junior-sized juleps served in old-fashioned glasses. Make with muddled sugar, ice cubes, and whiskey, gin, rum, or brandy, as well as sprigs of mint and a squirt of soda water, if desired, and garnish with fruit.

SOURS

Made with lemon juice, ice, sugar, and any of the basic liquors, these are tart lemony cocktails similar to a highly concentrated punch. Decorate with a lemon slice and cherry.

STRAWBERRY LIQUEUR DRINKS

STREGA DRINKS

SWEDISH PUNCH DRINKS

SWIZZLES

These drinks originally came from the West Indies where a swizzle stick is a twig having three to five forked branches on the end; it is inserted into the glass or pitcher and twirled rapidly between the hands. Tall, cool drinks of lime, sugar, liquor, bitters, and packed with shaved ice.

TODDIES

These may be served hot or cold. Dissolve a lump or teaspoon of sugar in a little water. Add liquor, ice, or hot water, and stir with clove, nutmeg, cinnamon, or lemon peel.

TRIPLE SEC DRINKS

VERMOUTH DRINKS

VODKA DRINKS

WHISKEY DRINKS
(Bourbon, Blended, Rye, or Canadian)

WINE DRINKS

Claret, Madeira, Muscatel,
Port, Rhine, Sauterne, Sherry,
White wine
(See Champagne Drinks on page 197)